"Regrets over yesterday and the fear of tomorrow
are twin thieves that rob us of the moment."

—AMISH PROVERB

WHISTLE STOP
Café
= MYSTERIES =

Under the Apple Tree
As Time Goes By
We'll Meet Again

# WE'LL MEET AGAIN

## JENELLE HOVDE

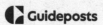
Guideposts

Whistle Stop Café Mysteries is a trademark of Guideposts.

Published by Guideposts Books & Inspirational Media
100 Reserve Road, Suite E200
Danbury, CT 06810
Guideposts.org

Cover and interior design by Müllerhaus
Cover illustration by Greg Copeland at Illustration Online LLC.
Typeset by Aptara, Inc.

ISBN 978-1-959634-25-6 (hardcover)
ISBN 978-1-959634-27-0 (epub)

Printed and bound in the United States of America
10 9 8 7 6 5 4 3 2 1

# WE'LL MEET AGAIN

Dedicated to my mother, Karen, and my father,
Jim Kelly. I'm so grateful for your love.
I can't wait until we meet again.

# GLOSSARY of AMISH TERMS

**bruder** • brother

**danki** • thank you

**daed** • father

**dawdi** • grandfather

**dochder** • daughter

**Englischer** • English or non-Amish

**Gelassenheit** • yielding or submission to the will of God

**Gott** • God

**grossmammi** • grandmother

**gut** • good

**kapp** • head covering

**liebling** • darling

**ja** • yes

**kuchen** • a pastry

**maam** • mother

**ne** • no

**oncle** • uncle

**Ordnung** • the written and unwritten rules of the Amish; the under-stood behavior by which the Amish are expected to live, passed down from generation to generation. These may differ slightly district to district.

**sohn** • son

**rumspringa** • rite of passage during adolescence for the Amish

**willkumme** • welcome

**wunderbaar** • wonderful

# CHAPTER ONE

*Dennison, Ohio*
*April 1943*

Oh, please, please let him like my gift.

*Ignoring the nervous flutter in her chest, Eileen Turner handed a wrapped package to the man who had stolen her heart. He loosened the string and peeled back the paper with a small cry.*

*"You bought me a book?" Samuel Lapp turned the blue volume over in his calloused hands. Gold lettering glinted in the sun as he examined the spine with an expression of something akin to awe.* The Odyssey *by Homer. His smile beamed far brighter than the elegant gilding. How tiny her gift looked, cradled in his long fingers.*

*She sucked in a quick breath, dazzled by that dimpled smile. Feigning nonchalance, she raised a* shoulder. "I know you wanted a copy, and I ordered it for you over a month ago."

He released a delighted laugh as he carefully opened the cover, the faint sound of crisp papers clinging to each other finally separating and breaking free. Gingerly, he flipped through the fragile pages edged with gold. She took advantage of the moment to observe him. Already, he was lost to her, his eyes rapidly skimming the words, his mind drinking them in like a man in desperate need of a soda pop on a sultry day.

And who would have thought Samuel Lapp, furniture maker extraordinaire and heir to Lapp Lumber, with his tanned arms beneath his rolled sleeves and his suspenders looped over his broad shoulders, would have such a keen desire for the written word? With the summer sun beating down, he pushed his straw hat up from his forehead, and his blond hair curled damp about his ears and neck from a morning of hard work. His mouth formed silent words as he continued to study Homer's writing.

She certainly didn't have the same insatiable desire to read. She had barely mustered a solid B in Mr. Hanson's English class, forcing herself to endure Shakespeare's Hamlet. To be, or not to be, that is the question. Well, if Mr. Hanson had asked her—and he hadn't—Hamlet proved pure agony, truth be told.

But making Samuel smile? It was worth the cost of the book plus the ninety-three-cent shipping-and-handling charges, all the way from Baker's Books in Columbus, Ohio.

She reached into her worn leather handbag and pulled out the second volume, feeling like she was about to dole out sarsaparilla sticks to the neighborhood kids. This book, The Rights of Man by Thomas Paine, had been hesitantly recommended by her papa.

When she slipped the books into her purse this morning, Papa had turned white around the gills. "Samuel isn't like us, sweetheart. I know you met him during his rumspringa, and he's been a special friend these past few years. But he's got a world he can't leave. Are you willing to abandon your way of life for him? Don't you give that boy false notions, you hear?"

"Eileen!" Samuel's cry broke through her thoughts, including Papa's chiding voice. "What have you done?"

She handed the book to him, her gloved fingers brushing his. A thrill rippled up her arm, aiming straight for her chest. And judging from the way his blue eyes startled, Samuel had felt the same electric spark.

"Eileen," he said again, this time with a hint of warning, "you should not have spent so much money on me."

"I know you can't get to the library easily, especially when barn-raising season comes," she said as
her cheeks flamed. "Besides, it's important to have
your own copy to read over and over again. You can
make notes in the margins and memorize the parts you
like best."

And think of me. Of course, she would not admit
that thought out loud.

He transferred both books to one arm and reached
for her hand, his thumb brushing across her knuckles.
Despite the fabric barrier of her uniform gloves, it felt
as though she wasn't wearing gloves at all. "You are so
gut to me. I cannot imagine my life before I met you,
and to think it has been three years. The best years I
can recall in a long time."

He raised her captured hand to his mouth, and...

Was he going to kiss her? Goodness, she just might
melt right into the lawn in Dennison's McCluskey Park
for all to see. Sure enough, he brushed his soft lips
against the back of her hand. Mercy.

"Samuel Lapp!" A strident voice shattered the ten-
der moment.

Eileen gulped as Samuel tore his gaze from hers to
look over her shoulder. His eyebrows dipped down-
ward in alarm, and he dropped her hand. She pivoted
on her sensible heels, only to witness a young man yank

on the reins of his black buggy, forcing it to a jerky halt on the road running parallel to the park.

"Oh no, it is Jacob," Samuel whispered. He edged past Eileen, the books pinned firmly beneath his arm. "It appears our date will be cut short."

The youth glared, squinting at Eileen as if she was a loathsome sight. Thinner, and with a ruddier complexion, Jacob looked like a younger, far more irritable version of Samuel. "Daed needs you back at the lumberyard. Why didn't you tell him you had plans to whittle away the afternoon?"

The look Samuel shot her was part regret, part resignation. He sighed. These stolen moments together seemed all too few these past months.

"It's okay. If you have to go, I understand. I've got to get back to the train station. Margot needs help with the sandwiches for the soldiers," she said. Although that wasn't entirely true. Margot had plenty of female volunteers ready to bat their eyelashes at the departing men who shipped out from the Dennison train station.

Besides, a more troubling thought took hold. Why hadn't Samuel told his family he was meeting her for lunch at the café? He had found a ride with his cousin, planning to deliver a hand-carved bench to Mrs. Healy, the first-grade teacher, and then meet Eileen. Was he ashamed to be caught with an Englischer?

Samuel glanced over his shoulder as he headed toward the buggy. "You know how my daed can get in a snit when I am not at the workshop. Hopefully, I will see you later. In two weeks at our special spot, ja?"

She nodded, her throat tightening at Samuel's sudden reserve. Though her handbag felt infinitely lighter, her heart sank. He climbed into the buggy, his jaw clenched, as Jacob's loud chiding rose in pitch. Then Jacob clucked his tongue while slapping the reins against the horses, and Samuel's solemn gaze sought hers.

Her afternoon ruined and her dignity in tatters, she adjusted her white gloves with the seed pearl buttons and headed toward the train station. Samuel's gentle touch lingered on her hands.

Perhaps Papa was right. Perhaps this connection with Samuel Lapp, one of the best furniture makers in all of Ohio's Amish country, might prove too risky in the end. Yet she felt drawn to his quiet strength, to his mysterious demeanor, and to the charming way he asked for her advice on Englischer ways. Didn't he seek her out when he came into town, never pressuring her for more than the pleasure of her company over a cup of coffee? Those visits had blossomed into something sweet and heady.

No, Samuel wasn't ashamed of her. She felt he cared deeply every time he found her in the train *station, flashing that winsome smile, his eyes alight when he saw her. His family? Well, that was another matter entirely.*

*Two weeks later, Eileen waited in McCluskey Park, shading her eyes as she searched the road for the famil-iar sight of a black buggy and chestnut workhorse. The sky overhead arched bright blue, and a young mother pushed a gray pram down the winding path, pausing every so often to coo to the baby nestled inside.*

*A tiny cry brought a pang to Eileen's chest as she furtively watched the woman reach into the pram and snuggle a small bundle of white. So many mothers and new brides faced long months of loneliness and uncer-tainty as their husbands left Dennison. Thousands of soldiers slipped through the train station, their hands outstretched for the canteen sandwiches and dough-nuts, now a famous treat served by the Salvation Army. Within less than a year, the train station had garnered nationwide attention. Beaming girls offered delicious food and one last glimpse of home as the men headed off to war. The GIs called Dennison* Dreamsville, USA, *in homage to Glenn Miller's song with the same name.*

*Eileen had received a coveted promotion after the previous stationmaster enlisted, and she loved the work—found purpose in it—but she also felt more tired than she could remember. The lunch dates with Samuel remained one bright spot, a chance to escape, even if for a moment. She shifted on the bench, glancing at the silver watch pinned to her dress. Twelve forty-five. No Samuel.*

*Her afternoon shift started in fifteen minutes. She had no choice but to return to the train station a few blocks away from the park. Disappointment sliced through her as she left. Had an accident occurred at the Lapp lumbermill? Or had Samuel's father finally put an end to their friendship? Samuel was twenty-one, only a year younger than she was. A man, by all accounts. Surely his father wouldn't continue to interfere?*

*With increasingly heavy steps, she hurried back to her post and the shifting train schedules and never-ending maintenance issues that demanded her attention. But neither her duties nor the low rumble of the engines and the steady stream of travelers could distract her, and after her shift ended, she continued to mull over what had happened to Samuel. He rarely canceled.*

*That evening, when she entered the house, a pile of letters lay scattered across the kitchen table. Bless*

Papa, he tried so hard to help her. Some days he retrieved the mail from the post office, but other days he forgot.

"Is that you, Eileen?" her father called from the living room.

"Yes, Papa. It's me," she answered as she hung her hat on the coatrack in the hallway and tugged her gloves free. She cast them onto the console against the wall.

She peeked around the corner. He sat in an overstuffed club chair, unfolding a newspaper with a rattle. With his leg propped up on a tufted footstool, he appeared the picture of comfort. But she knew that leg ached something fierce from an old wound courtesy of the First World War. A breeze ruffled the living room curtains, a few of the windows opened despite the afternoon heat. Already her dress clung to her skin, thanks to the humidity in the stifling room. Perhaps he hurt too much to get up and close the windows.

"There's a letter for you in the kitchen. Samuel Lapp, I believe," he said.

Her pulse skittered as she recognized the bold scrawl. After tearing open the envelope, she pulled out a sheet of blue-lined paper, the kind a child would use during his grammar lessons.

Eileen,

I read the books you gave me. Read them twice, in fact. I have never received a gift that so spoke to my soul. I cannot help but think that *Gott* placed you in my life for a reason. Every night, I sleep with the books on my nightstand, and I dream of you.

Daed wanted to burn the books, but I would not let him. I fear the neighbors heard our horrible fight three days ago. I cringe, thinking of it. I said hard things to him, things a good *sohn* should never say. He is a decent man and deserves far better than rebellion, but he does not understand my need to read and see more of the world. You do, however. And with you, I feel more alive than I have ever felt.

I have been thinking about many things since our last meeting. This dreadful business with Germany and the brave men who ship overseas to protect their hurting brothers and fight for the freedom to think and worship as one pleases, to exist fully as our Creator intended. *The Rights of Man* challenged me to my very core. Long ago, my people fled persecution hoping to find religious freedom.

Why should I not fight for those I love? Why should I not fight for you and everyone else in Dennison? There. I said it. I wanted to say it to you before Jacob rudely interrupted us. But I love you,

Eileen. I will always love you, my *liebling*. From the moment I bumped into you on my rumspringa, knocking the ice cream cone right out of your hand, I was smitten. There you stood at the soda counter, wearing that pink dress. And clumsy oaf that I was, I nearly trampled your shoes. But you merely laughed when you saw the ice cream staining your outfit. Not at me—just the situation. I thought you had the prettiest laugh, like little bells tinkling in a row. And you even let me replace your double vanilla scoop, suggesting I try the chocolate sprinkles on top.

Was that our first date? Listening to the Mills Brothers sing from the radio while eating ice cream from the Revco Drugstore? I felt like I had tasted heaven. How I looked forward to being with you, snatching moments dancing to Sinatra, with my arms wrapped around you as you pressed your cheek against mine. These things I had remained blissfully unaware of until I met you. You changed me, Eileen. And now, like Odysseus of *The Odyssey*, I find I am embarking on a journey of doing what is right and noble. How it fires my imagination!

*She lowered the paper, tears blurring the rest of the black letters, slanted and bold, telling her of his plans. Why had she ever thought to offer him those books, of all choices? Never in her wildest imagining would she have pictured him, a conscientious objector, leaving his family and business behind to fight overseas in France, or wherever the Good Lord would send him.*

*How could she possibly say goodbye to the man who had meant everything to her? Yet... Papa had fretted Samuel would reject her for the plain life. She had wrestled with whether she would fit in with the Amish community, abandoning her favorite music and all she held dear. Because of her, Samuel had held off on baptism, signaling his hesitance to embrace his Amish heritage.*

*Was this God's plan? To change him and, somehow, bring them closer in the end?*

*If so, why this path, Lord?*

*She sensed no discernible answer to that prayer other than the cooing of a mourning dove settled in the nearby oak tree just outside the kitchen window. As she headed to the living room, two thoughts battled, each one fighting for dominance as she clutched the precious letter to her chest.*

*He loved her! And he was leaving.*

# CHAPTER TWO

**D**ebbie Albright held her breath as she checked the oven one last time. The shiny stainless steel bore evidence of a Monday morning's hard work, with flour fingerprints smudged everywhere. She hated a dirty kitchen, but the Amish whoopie pies presented a new challenge to be conquered. If Janet hadn't talked her into making the delicate cookies, she'd be cracking the quarter rolls into the cash register by now.

"You look like you lost the war with the mixer." Janet Shaw's chipper voice rang out from behind Debbie. Debbie groaned, refusing to take her eyes off the small circles rising from the parchment paper.

She finally met her friend's gaze as Janet walked toward her with a to-go cup of steaming coffee in each hand. "You said this would be a moneymaker."

Janet set one cup on the counter and took a sip from the other. Debbie had suggested they sleep in after a busy week, and Janet looked well rested. "Whoopie pies *are* moneymakers. Yours were perfection last week. You just need to believe in yourself when you whip that batter. How's the filling?"

The filling was truly wonderful—a confection of shortening slowly blended with vanilla and sugar until it was as smooth and rich as any buttercream. Once the chocolate cookies cooled, they would pipe the filling on half of them then sandwich a second one on top of each.

Debbie eyed the cup on the counter and sighed. Janet's latest experiment in specialty coffee would have to wait. "The filling isn't half bad. And everyone loves chocolate, right?"

Janet leaned against the counter, eyeing her. "Relax. Our baking made the front page of the *Gazette*. As long as we keep adding new items to the menu, our customers will return. One day we'll make it onto Ohio's tourism list for scrumptious desserts."

Hopefully. The venture of running a café had been a lifelong dream. What better place than Dennison's historic train station? The Whistle Stop Café attracted tourists, but it also offered a relaxing gathering place for the close-knit community to connect over coffee, baked goods, and savory lunch fare.

Debbie slid her hands into a pair of baking mitts, opened the oven door, and retrieved the pan. The edges of the cookies had baked to a perfect crisp.

"No lumps or bumps on the surface." Janet nodded her approval. She pinched a piece of a cookie from the parchment paper. "Oh, hot, hot!" Despite the heat, her face beamed as soon as she popped the bite into her mouth.

Debbie held her breath.

"Divine." Janet's dreamy sigh was compliment enough. "If I'm ever too sick to bake, I know who I'll call."

Debbie chuckled. She much preferred crunching numbers and managing the day-to-day aspects of the café to fighting with the oven. And she liked cooking delicious meals better than baking crumbling pastries. But offering Janet a rare break was completely worth it. Brushing her fingers against her striped apron, Debbie snuck a peek at the clock. Six thirty. They had plenty of time to pipe the filling and maybe even whip up some extra blackberry scones.

Being free to create proved a treat. A week ago, Debbie had framed vintage posters of Uncle Sam and Rosie the Riveter to place on the walls, the colorful art complementing the train station's history of transporting soldiers during World War II. Visitors from all over the United States, and some from even as far as England, came to visit the depot and absorb the history. In time, they could make the Whistle Stop a premier café, depending on Janet's baking and Debbie's management and marketing skills.

Debbie rolled her tight shoulders to ease the tension she felt right down to the tip of her toes. In the last couple of weeks, she had dipped into her hard-earned savings to oversee historically accurate renovations to the café. Who knew wainscoting and beadboard could prove so expensive? Or the historical society so difficult to impress?

*Please, Lord, let this week be a success.* A common enough prayer these days.

Janet drained the last of her coffee before tossing the cup into the nearest trash can. "Thank you for insisting I sleep in for an extra hour. All right, put me to work." Dressed casually in beige cargo pants, comfy sneakers, and a pink T-shirt that read KEEP CALM AND EAT A CUPCAKE, she reached for another striped apron hanging from a hook on the kitchen wall.

Debbie grinned. Her hair was about to escape her ponytail, and powdered sugar splotched her slim khaki jeans and black running shoes. She certainly looked a mess compared to Janet. Not that she minded the differences between them. She would be forever grateful that her dear friend had agreed to co-run the Whistle Stop Café.

Janet peered at the oven. "The cookies need to cool, or the filling will melt and puddle. Why don't you take the cake pops out of the fridge and set them in the display case?"

Debbie saluted before opening the fridge, a stainless-steel monstrosity that had cost far too much, considering the stretched budget. She carefully pulled out the nearest tray of vanilla truffle cake pops dipped in white chocolate and sprinkled with red sugar crystals.

The cake pops always sold well, especially when kids rushed into the café following the scenic train rides. The station now offered a day camp for students. Beginning this week, children would absorb the history of the museum and be treated to a special train ride after lunch. Debbie loved seeing their round faces and sticky hands smooshed against the curved glass of the display cabinet, eyes big with wonder over the variety of baked goods. She just didn't enjoy cleaning up the mess later. Thankfully, they had hired Annie Butler, a college student from Ohio State, to give them a hand for the late summer rush.

As Debbie set her tray on the counter, the overhead fluorescent lights flickered and popped off. She flipped a nearby light switch, but nothing happened.

"Power's out!" she called over her shoulder.

Janet burst through the door and groaned. The café, which sat at the end of the same train depot where the wartime volunteers served sandwiches to thousands of departing soldiers, lay in sweltering darkness. The only light filtered through the curtained windows.

"Did a breaker trip?" Janet asked. "I can't imagine why something like this would happen. We aren't pulling that much power this morning."

Debbie peered out the nearest window and viewed the street in front of the train station. The parking lot, freshly painted with bright yellow lines, lay mostly empty. With the sunrise just peeking over the trees, the streetlights remained dark. She wasn't sure if they should be on or not. She recognized Kim Smith's vehicle, parked in its usual spot. Kim always came to the train station early in the morning. And, as the director of the museum, she was usually the last person in the evening to leave. Only one other vehicle, a sleek, black Jaguar, waited near the copse of trees, on the other end of the lot.

That wasn't something Debbie saw every day in Dennison. Why was such an expensive car parked near the depot so early in the morning?

She turned away from the window, letting the curtain fall back into place. "Kim's here. Maybe we can ask her to reset the breaker. I can't tell if the power is out for the rest of the street."

Janet nodded, her lips pinched tight. But before Debbie could leave the café, the door swung open and Kim came in, her short chestnut hair mussed. She pushed a pair of tortoiseshell glasses up the bridge of her nose and took a deep breath. Her uniform, a 1940s-styled suit complete with brown heels, made her look like she had stepped out of a Frank Sinatra movie. Usually, she saved the vintage outfits for special presentations about Dennison's wartime history, and her holiday uniforms brought plenty of community buzz.

Kim glanced around the room. "Power out for you too?"

Debbie nodded. "Yep. And not a storm in sight."

Kim rubbed her hands together. "Right. I need to check the breaker, and I also wanted to ask you…"

Janet raised an eyebrow. "Yes?"

Kim dropped her voice to a stage whisper. "There's a man out front. He's been walking around the building for about fifteen minutes now. It's strange. I almost went out to tell him that the museum and ticket booth won't open until eight thirty, but the sign says it so clearly. And when I arrived this morning, I found the back door to the station unlocked. I need to find out who left it open. I'm hoping we don't have a careless construction worker renovating the newest bed-and-breakfast car."

Over the summer Kim had arranged for a grant from the esteemed National Trust for Historic Preservation Society to purchase a second Pullman car to offer additional accommodations for tourists. The project had taken far longer than she had estimated, pushing the opening date of the second Pullman car to possibly later in the fall.

Janet tensed. "We locked the café yesterday. And we don't use your back entrance. Do you want help when you check the breaker? I could hold the flashlight for you. There isn't much we can do in the kitchen without power."

Kim opened the café door to go back out into the large open space that used to house the depot waiting area. "I'll text my electrician if we can't get the power up and running. Surely we don't have a problem with the wiring. It was one of the first things we replaced when we began restorations."

As the resident historian, Kim was responsible for the train station's listing with the National Register of Historic Places. Debbie was glad the depot was on the register, but the listing meant that upgrades to the building had to maintain the original features whenever possible.

Debbie shook her head as Janet and Kim left for the breaker board in the storage room. On a whim, she headed to the same café window where she had first spied the black Jaguar. She pulled the checkered curtain back with one finger. The purple dawn had disappeared as golden sunlight flooded the parking lot. Sure enough, the same black car remained parked next to the trees.

A man walked past the building, looking over his shoulder.

Debbie yelped and covered her mouth, and then she chuckled. Why was she so jumpy? Surely he was just another tourist, albeit one who had arrived well before opening. She took a deep breath to steady her nerves and peered out a third time. He hurried toward the tracks, his hands jammed into his navy pants pockets. The wind played with his sandy hair, tousling his unruly curls.

She watched a moment longer, noting how he stood in the parking lot as if debating what to do. Then he headed south, following the train tracks leading out of town.

*Weird.*

As Debbie turned away from the window, Janet entered the room, face flushed. "When the power goes, the central air goes. It's like a furnace in that storage room with enough humidity to make a steam bath."

Clearly, tripping the breaker hadn't worked. "Is a line down?"

Janet nodded. "Kim's on it. She called the power company. Our electrician, Mark, will arrive in twenty minutes or so." She sighed as she checked her watch. "Let's pray the worst-case scenario doesn't happen."

Debbie inhaled deeply. "Thanks for the reminder to pray." Nothing easily ruffled Janet, a quality Debbie wouldn't mind adopting.

Janet pointed to the forgotten paper cup. "At least you can finish your coffee. I brought it from home. Try it and tell me we don't need a French press here at the café. It's a café Viennoise. Next week I'll bring a café Cubano and a Yuanyang."

"A *what*?"

"Just try it! You're holding an espresso mixed with rich cream, frothy milk, and a hint of cocoa—my addition. Very popular in Budapest, from what I've heard. So, take that cup, sit down, and relax for a minute."

Relax? A wishful dream. As Janet covered the frosting bowl with plastic wrap, Debbie picked up the cup, already cool to the touch, and took a sip of the tepid yet delicious brew before eyeing the windows lining the front of the café. "By the way, that guy—the one Kim was talking about? I just saw him. I think he's the owner of the Jaguar. He moved south, walking next to the tracks."

Janet tightened the loose strings of her apron. "A tourist, maybe? Or a historian? You know how dedicated those amateur historians are to their research." She winked at Debbie before heading into the kitchen.

Debbie chuckled as she cradled the lukewarm cup in her hands. Kim certainly loved history, spending every available minute interviewing the town's older citizens, especially those who had survived World War II. Dennison had plenty of amateur historians. She supposed one more wouldn't hurt. She was about to savor another sip of coffee when the door to the café banged against the wall. Debbie groaned. That section of wainscotting was taking a beating.

Kim rushed into the café, wide eyed. "My office has been raided!"

# CHAPTER THREE

*D*ebbie rushed alongside Kim to the office, Janet following close behind. Early morning light highlighted Kim's work area, including a large oak desk strewn with papers. A comfy club chair sat against the wall, and a series of brass lamps brought a coziness to the space.

Kim pointed to the desk. "I've been cataloging historic kitchen items, including several pieces used by the Salvation Army during the war effort. I had grouped a section to be put on display for the café. I can't find them anywhere!"

Kim had recently suggested finding a curio cabinet to fill with vintage canisters, teacups, bread boxes, butter molds, potato mashers, and an assortment of nesting pastry cutters. Guests could view the items while waiting to be seated.

Debbie had loved the idea, and her mother had enthusiastically donated a 1940s serving tray advertising Southern Dairies Sealtest Ice Cream. The tray was still in good shape, with yellow enamel and black trim. Debbie remembered when her grandmother used the tray to serve fresh-baked cookies. Mom had thought the item would provide the perfect inspiration for her two favorite café owners.

Debbie looked at the desktop, where papers were carelessly pushed to the side. Kim picked up a potato masher with a worn wooden handle. "I said that the back door was unlocked this morning. Well, so was my office door. I didn't think anything of that, because sometimes I forget to lock it. But it looks like someone has been in here. I had an egg beater and an enamelware ladle right here on the desk. Now they're gone!"

"Did Silas come in here to clean last night?" Janet asked.

Kim had hired Silas Yoder as temporary custodian to help with the summer traffic. He was an older man in his sixties who prefered to keep as busy as possible.

"Silas knows he's not to touch my workspace. No, I'm missing several kitchen utensils, including a Dazey Ice Crusher and a pamphlet for the Doughnut Corporation of America. Did you know the Doughnut Corporation sold many of their machines to servicemen who started their own doughnut stores? The pamphlet shows a soldier returning from the war to start his business. I'm not happy about losing this, considering all the soldiers who passed through our station and received free doughnuts and coffee. I planned on framing that pamphlet for display."

Debbie studied the contents on the desk again. "I'm so sorry, Kim. I can't imagine who would take it."

Kim shook her head, her lips pinched tightly together. "I even had a complete sterling silver cutlery set with forks, knives, and spoons from 1941. It was a wedding gift donated by a local family. I spent months curating those items. Your grandmother's tray is also missing."

Debbie gasped. Her mother would be so disappointed to hear the news. "Oh no."

Kim's troubled gaze met Debbie's. "Yes. And I was going to tell you today that I did some research on it last night. It's worth nearly three hundred dollars. Maybe more."

Shocked, Debbie could only stare at her friend. "Did I hear you right? Mom and I had no idea."

Kim sighed. "Most people don't know what these pieces are worth. It can be surprising to see the price of vintage teacups or quilts online. One thing's for sure. Someone knows their value. Who would do this?"

Debbie mulled over Kim's question for the next half hour while waiting for Mark Thomas, their electrician and general handyman, to show up. Kim also called Ian, Janet's husband and the police chief of Dennison, to discuss the missing items even though there was no sign of an intruder.

Debbie's thoughts were interrupted when Mark entered the café, his crewcut still glistening as if he had recently hopped out of the shower. Debbie gave him a quick hug. "Thanks for coming, Mark. We're so sorry to pull you away from your baby girl. How's Becky doing?"

"It's no problem. I'll be happy to look at the breaker. Especially if you think someone messed with it." Mark grinned as he hefted his tool kit. "Since you asked, we've had nothing but sleepless nights, endless diapers, and plenty of takeout. You should see our little Abby. The doctor said she gained two pounds last week."

"I'll come as soon as I can," Kim promised, smiling. "You tell Becky to rest." Becky was Kim's cousin's daughter, and they were close.

Debbie couldn't help but smile at the new father's enthusiasm. She was grateful for any distraction from the tension regarding power outages, lost revenue, and missing antiques. Plus, Becky had offered wonderful advice on the café's redecoration, providing the free service as a gift to Kim. The young mother had recently started an interior-design business, specializing in the rustic farmhouse look.

"Sounds like somebody has Daddy wrapped around her little finger," Debbie said. "I can't wait to see her. Hopefully, you and Becky will get a good night's rest soon."

Mark's smile slipped a notch. "Well, truthfully, Abby isn't the only reason Becky is losing sleep. We just found out one of her clients might cancel a project. A few months ago she placed a big order for Amish furniture, and the store owner, Daniel Lapp, had to delay delivery for some reason. Now Daniel claims he never received the order for the second bedroom—a bed, dresser, nightstands, and a wardrobe. He blames Becky for the miscommunication and is raising the price for the additional furniture. Despite the down payment, he won't deliver the pieces until Becky pays in full. Now Becky's clients want to end their contract with her and get their money back."

"Good grief," Kim said as she opened the door that led into the hall. "What a shame. I heard Daniel Lapp is a tough man to work with, even if he makes some of the finest furniture around, like his father did. Just goes to show, even if you inherit a business, you can't rest on past accolades."

Mark grunted, no doubt keeping his thoughts to himself. A poor reputation was next to impossible to shake in a small town—a misfortune Debbie prayed she'd never experience with the café.

"I didn't expect my wife to lose a huge contract," Mark said. "It couldn't come at a worse time for us. Becky and I want to buy a house this year. We've been saving every penny we can. I don't know how we'll be able to offer a decent down payment by the end of the year."

"That's unfortunate," Debbie said. "Maybe Daniel will reconsider."

Kim snorted as she edged into the shadowed hall while holding the door open. "Not likely. I've always known the men at Lapp Lumber to be stubborn."

Mark took the hint to get to work, but Debbie couldn't leave him so downcast. She touched his sleeve just as he brushed past her. "I'll bring a casserole tonight. No more fast food for you two. I'm certain that would be the doctor's orders."

Mark smiled. "I'll never turn down food from the Whistle Stop Café."

Debbie blew out a breath when Kim and Mark disappeared into the hallway. Janet cleared her throat. "Back to Kim's office. Is it possible someone misplaced the items? Maybe Silas?"

Debbie shrugged. "I guess it's possible. But I can't think of any reason why Silas would move them."

Janet sighed. "Honestly, I feel for Kim. Her job can't be an easy one. I'm sure your grandmother's tray will turn up soon. Hopefully someone just thought the things needed to be moved."

"I know Mom will be sad to hear about what happened. What else is going to fall apart this morning?" Debbie frowned as she moved to the door and ran her fingers across the scarred wainscoting. "We may need to repair some of this woodwork. It's taken quite a beating in the last two months. One more expense to add to our list."

"I've stashed a spare fund to cover some of these expenses." Janet patted Debbie's arm. "We're in this together, right?"

"Well, yes. We are in this together. I'm just worried we're going to run into more repairs than we can handle."

Janet's expression softened, and she tucked a strand of hair behind her ear. "If God brought us this far with the café, I don't think He'll abandon us in our hour of need. We've got to trust Him with these concerns. And He'll take care of Becky's and Kim's issues too. You'll see."

Debbie nodded. The reminder of God's provision couldn't have been timelier, especially when she remembered she'd left a draining corporate job that involved untenable work hours and stressful commuting in congested traffic. For nearly twenty years, she had felt alone in the city, keeping herself occupied with work. Dennison was a haven, offering her a chance to rebuild her life into healthier rhythms and reconnect with old friends. Janet, despite her no-nonsense attitude, was an encourager and a protector. They had grown up together, attending the same high school as best friends, and Debbie knew her friend's reminders were genuine.

Maybe she was being a bit melodramatic. As Janet often stated, Debbie couldn't predict or control everything. Of course, she tried her best to manage painful outcomes....

The overhead fluorescent lights hummed and flickered to life eight minutes before opening. Debbie cheered, and Janet shook her wooden spoon in triumph. Debbie had eyed the gathering customers nervously as the minutes ticked by on the oversized clock hanging above a nearby booth. She had placed printed signs on many of the windows, indicating they were hoping to open on time. Janet remained convinced the power would return.

Thankfully, the morning hadn't been a complete loss. They'd placed the filled whoopie pies neatly in trays beneath the glass counter. Janet retrieved additional stored baked goods from the previous night while Debbie updated the enormous chalkboard menu on the wall and then checked the coffee percolating beside the rows of sugared syrups. The fresh scent of hazelnut and a golden Hawaiian brew mingled with all the other wonderful smells of the kitchen.

The restaurant door creaked, catching Debbie's attention. Annie crept inside the kitchen, her normally cheerful face wearing a frown. She jabbed her thumb toward the front door. "What's with all the signs? Is something wrong?"

"The power was out. It came on a few minutes ago though." Debbie waved a roll of quarters. "Want to prep the register while I take the signs down?"

Annie had proven a tremendous blessing this past month, filling in as needed. But, as a college student, her days at the Whistle Stop Café would soon end. When she had asked for a job, Debbie had readily agreed. It was tough to find experienced help. Annie had flipped burgers part-time in a food court at Ohio State University. Plus, she was staying in Dennison with her father and teenage brother, Nicholas. Debbie liked to offer work to the town's residents and give back whenever she could, especially to a college student with so much on her plate.

The young woman pulled on her apron and hurried to the register. She tossed her blond braid over her shoulder and started opening rolls of coins. "It's going to be a madhouse. I don't think I've ever counted so many cars in the parking lot."

"Extra tips," Janet said as she placed the last tray of cookies in the display case. "We could all use a little extra this week."

Annie opened the cash drawer, its answering ring a cheerful sound. "Perfect. I told Nicholas I'd spring for supper tomorrow night at Buona Vita. We've both been craving some good pizza."

Janet smiled. "Good choice. They are excellent."

Annie closed the cash drawer and gathered the paper from the coins. "I've been meaning to ask you all. Do you think I would enjoy the train ride they're offering with the day camp?"

Debbie smiled as she listened to Janet and Annie discuss the current Victory Tour schedule that involved museum stops and wonderful scenery with just the right hint of historic charm.

She glanced at Janet. "Nothing beats the Christmas rides though. Am I right?"

Janet fixed her hairnet, her expression dreamy. "No, nothing beats the Christmas rides. I still remember them from when I was a little girl. My grandfather used to take me each year as a part of our family's Christmas tradition. He told me the journey was real and that if I was lucky, I'd make it to the North Pole. Of course, he would pretend we'd arrived at the Arctic when the elves entered the cars with buckets of candy canes. I loved to pretend with him."

Debbie was about to say more when Mark popped into view. "Good news, ladies. I've discovered the saboteur."

Annie paused. "Saboteur?"

Debbie's heart thudded to a stop. A picture of the stranger and his Jaguar came into her mind's view along with Kim's flustered behavior, no power, and missing antiques.

A teasing glint shone from Mark's eyes. "I'm kidding. I made a call and learned that a transformer on Bell Street blew. You can thank the central power guys for fixing it. I'll be back to replace some of the older fluorescent lights that shorted out in the hallways. I've got to run to the hardware store, but you should be able to bake."

Janet tugged her apron strings tighter. "There are some things missing from Kim's office. Did you happen to see a box of vintage kitchen utensils anywhere?"

Mark shrugged. "I didn't. Does it look like someone broke in?"

"No," said Janet. "Both the back door and Kim's office door were unlocked this morning, but there was no damage to either one."

While Janet wrote out a check, Mark eyed the cookies in the trays. "I'll take a few of those, please."

Debbie reached into the glass display case and grabbed the largest sugar cookies and a few of the whoopie pies. She slid them into a paper bag and gave it to Mark, who beamed as he handed her his credit card.

"Just make sure you save some treats for Becky," Janet teased.

"Always," he said as he took his credit card back.

"So the power outage was a city problem." Janet raised an eyebrow after Mark exited the front door. She clucked her tongue. "I'm relieved."

Debbie stretched her arms and willed the tension to release from her aching muscles. Janet was right. She really ought to pray more over these situations, no matter how big or small, and let God figure out the rest.

Annie closed the register drawer after storing the receipt from Mark's purchase. "What's this I hear about stolen antiques?"

Janet polished a finger smudge on the glass display with her sleeve. "Kim thinks someone got into her office and stole some items. She said the back door, the one closest to her office, was left open. Someone must have forgotten to lock up last night. I know we locked our side, so it wasn't us."

Fingering her braid, Annie's brow pinched with concentration. "That's true. I saw you lock up, Janet."

"Silas or Kim usually locks the station," Debbie offered, hoping to reassure her friends. Did she really need another mystery to solve? She had plenty of work to focus on this morning.

By the time late afternoon came and they closed their doors for the day, Debbie was more than ready to take a breather. She stepped outside the train station for fresh air. The whistles shrieked and the engines hissed as the last train prepared for its final round trip.

A vaguely familiar face flashed from the crowd of eager tourists. She recognized the same man from the early-morning hours. He seemed to be looking for someone. He certainly didn't look weird anymore. In fact, he appeared…lost. When the students boarded the train, he remained next to a bench pushed against the station wall. Debbie slipped back into the station before he noticed her watching him.

What was he waiting for? Or perhaps, *who* was he waiting for? She couldn't speculate too long on the questions when she had a café to run. She and Annie sped through their daily cleanup tasks, and Debbie couldn't help feeling a swell of satisfaction when Janet declared that not a single whoopie pie remained.

A successful day, considering the way it had begun.

Debbie breathed a sigh of relief as she poured one last cup of coffee to take with her. Janet had whipped up a casserole during a short lull in the action, and it was all packaged and waiting for delivery to Becky and Mark.

"Want to come with me to Lapp Lumber Wednesday afternoon after we close up for the day?" Janet asked as she lifted her purse from the desk that served as a mini office.

Debbie propped her fists on her hips. "You bet I'll be there, asking my nosy questions."

"Of course you will."

A grin spread across Annie's face, and she coughed. It was obvious to Debbie she did it to hide a snicker. "Go ahead and leave early on Wednesday, ladies. I can manage the stragglers who linger over their lunches, and close up shop."

Debbie paused, reluctant to place her new employee in such a role of responsibility. But she couldn't deny that she really wanted to find out more about the Lapp men. And Kim would be close by. "I suppose we could do that. You'll have Kim here for help if you have an emergency."

"Did you see that guy with the Jaguar again?" Janet asked as she slung the strap of her purse over her shoulder.

"I did. I'm sure he's gone by now. He must have been waiting for someone most of the day." Debbie took another sip of coffee. She really needed to leave the caffeine for the morning, but she didn't think she'd be able to stay awake through supper without a boost of energy. "You two go on, and I'll be right behind you. I'm going to get a couple of sides for Mark and Becky's supper."

After Janet and Annie left, Debbie boxed up some salad and blueberry scones to go with the casserole, packed it all in a cooler, and gathered her purse. She exited the station, locked the depot door, and then turned and saw the neatly dressed stranger leaning against his Jaguar with his phone in hand.

As Debbie walked to her car, the man raised his head, his gaze colliding with hers for the briefest second. He hesitated as she raised her hand to wave. But before she could call out a greeting to him, he unlocked his car and ducked inside. A moment later, the car revved to life and peeled out of the parking lot.

# CHAPTER FOUR

While she was trying to make heads or tails out of the man's action, Debbie spied Silas Yoder entering the parking lot for his Monday evening shift. Normally, he waited until after business hours to clean the building, working late in the evening. His long gray hair, caught in a ponytail, and rugged jeans paired with a faded Aerosmith T-shirt gave him an old rock-and-roller vibe.

Debbie liked him. His knowledge of seventies' rock musicians remained unparalleled, and she knew he was lonely. He had older grandchildren in Columbus, but they only visited Dennison occasionally. His personal history—well, seemed rather sketchy. Silas had a unique ability to deflect personal questions, especially ones dealing with his service in Vietnam.

"Hey, Silas." She waved as he approached, walking his bike. "You're early today. Did you hear the news about the missing antiques from Kim's office?"

He startled then relaxed. His keys jingled from a large ring attached to his belt loop, creating music with every step. He rested his rugged mountain bike—a donated gift—against the wall of the station. Silas had gone through hard times, and Kim had offered the job to help him following a devastating bankruptcy. As an army veteran, he continued to claim benefits, but he also needed a steady job. It kept him busy and out of trouble, he had shared with Debbie over coffee at the café one day.

"If you've got questions about her office, I'm as puzzled as you are," he said. He brushed the keys at his side, as if to reassure himself they remained on the ring. "I came early to check on the train cars, especially the newest Pullman undergoing repairs. None of the workers have seen any misplaced antiques. It doesn't explain how someone got into the station. I always lock up, Debbie."

The strain in his voice touched her. "No one is blaming you, Silas. We locked up as well. I remember Janet jiggling the door handle just to make sure."

His mouth pulled down into a harsh line. "Kim is worried. I just know she's going to blame me for it, even though I know she frequently leaves her door unlocked. I'm not the one who left the door open, and I need this job."

His voice boomed louder than usual. *Is he wearing his hearing aids?* She discreetly eyed his ears where the small beige aids peeked out. Sometimes the batteries died, and if so, Silas's hearing muffled significantly.

Pivoting on his heel before she could say anything more, he let himself into the building, muttering something about needing to wash the windows.

Debbie knew Silas's complaint was true—Kim hardly ever locked her office during work hours and was always darting in and out, taking care of business. As museum curator, she had so much to manage between the displays, the employees, and museum volunteers. She had worked late into the evening the past few weeks, preparing educational presentations for the upcoming school year when students from all across the area would be bused in to learn about World War II history. And then there were the government grants to write, requesting funds and justifying costs….

Poor Kim. When would she get a break?

As she drove home, Debbie couldn't help but hope her friends might come to a better understanding.

At suppertime, Debbie knocked on one of the cranberry-painted doors of a gingerbread Victorian-era house converted into a series of small but charming apartments. The door opened, and Becky, her brown hair caught in a loose bun, greeted Debbie with a smile. "Mark told me you were bringing dinner."

Debbie lifted the cooler. "Well, it was Janet who actually made the casserole. I'm just the delivery girl."

Becky laughed and waved Debbie inside a hall lined with floral wallpaper and white baseboards. "I'm drooling already. If you brought food, I hope you stay to eat with us. Mark should be home in a few minutes. I just put Abby down for a much-needed nap."

The invitation warmed Debbie. She followed Becky to an old-fashioned parlor with a gorgeous marble fireplace. Everything appeared tastefully decorated, from the tufted leather sofa placed in front of the bay window and a series of barrister bookshelves to the oversized farmhouse table flanked with benches. "Thanks, I can't stay long. I'm only here to drop off the food. I've got to do some work in my house, and frankly, I'm running out of hours in the day, even with my dad's help." Debbie's recently retired father had been eager to assist with her needed projects.

Becky groaned as she led the way to the kitchen. "Don't I know it? I'm sure your house will be stunning when it's finished."

"I may need some of your decorating advice. I'd love to keep the craftsman style as accurate as I can." She had purchased her house from Ray Zink, a decorated World War II veteran and current resident of the Good Shepherd Retirement Center. She adored every inch of her new home, from the plastered walls and rippled panes of window glass to the oak trim and paneling throughout the parlor and the dining room. The built-in cupboards provided plenty of storage. A few of the original chandeliers with tarnished brass and frosted glass remained. A stained glass window on the stair landing offered a cheerful glow of red and green.

Unfortunately, replacing the old knob and tube wiring had cost more than she had expected, but Mark had proven very helpful in rewiring the old home.

Becky lifted the foil from the casserole and inhaled deeply. "You bought a real gem of a house. Do you know how hard it is to find a historic craftsman with the original details still intact?"

Debbie sensed the perfect opportunity to broach a delicate subject. "Mark shared you're looking to buy a house. How's the search going?"

Becky's face fell as she pulled plates from the cupboard. "I don't know what all Mark told you, but we might have to put our dream of buying a house on hold. I've got a very irate customer who wanted to have a house full of Amish furniture. I don't know what happened, but Daniel Lapp insists I never ordered certain pieces, and now I'm hearing about quite a delay. I'm sure I remember him writing the order."

"Do you have a copy of the order?" Debbie asked.

Becky flushed. "That's just it. I don't remember what I did with the papers. The rumors about pregnancy brain—or more accurately, tired-mom brain—are true. I've looked everywhere, and I can't find that slip in my records. Somehow, I've got to deliver a rustic interior for a family of six. New house and construction completed by Greg Connor. I know he didn't have any issues with Lapp Lumber. For me, it's been a completely different story. I can barely get Daniel to talk to me. It's not like I can call him on the phone."

Debbie knew Greg. He had his own construction company and had proven to be an invaluable resource for her as she renovated her home. He was also an attractive widower with two teenage sons—a fact that his mother, Paulette, hinted at occasionally when waitressing at the café.

"So Greg got the lumber just fine from the Lapps, but you didn't receive your order of furniture?"

Becky sighed. "Exactly. And from what I've heard, Lapp Lumber does quality work. I remember going over the details of the furniture I needed with them. Daniel specifically asked me about the number of nightstands. So how did this mix-up happen? If I don't get that order completed on time, my reputation as a designer will be on the line."

"Would you like Janet or me to mention the situation to Daniel? We need to talk to him about replacing some trim and a section of beadboard at the café. Maybe we could nudge him to talk to you."

Becky fiddled with the aluminum foil crumpled beside the casserole before raising her troubled gaze to meet Debbie's. "Thanks for the offer. It's very kind of you. I don't think you'll get far with Daniel though. He insists I never ordered the additional furniture. He's as stubborn as stubborn comes. But I won't turn down any extra help."

# CHAPTER FIVE

The scent of apples and cinnamon greeted Debbie Tuesday morning when she unlocked the Whistle Stop Café door. A vibrant sunrise peeked above the rustling trees, promising yet another beautiful day. She shut the door behind her and inhaled the delicious aroma wafting from the kitchen.

Janet must be in the back, baking something marvelous. Debbie's stomach growled in anticipation as she hurried through the dining room. "What magic is this? I've never smelled anything so heavenly."

"I hear it's called *kuchen*." A familiar masculine voice came from a booth next to the kitchen.

Debbie spun to see Greg Connor sitting at the table with a mug. He waved sheepishly. "Sorry, didn't mean to scare you. Janet promised to bake for my crew this morning. I came early for a cup of coffee."

She laughed and set her purse on the counter with a plunk. "I take it you're waiting for the kuchen." Of course, he was here for the construction crew, wearing that black T-shirt and those dark-rinse jeans, which appeared to be his standard work uniform. The spicy cologne was new though. And the tousled hair.

He smiled, his cheeks dimpling in the most charming way. "I'm also interested in muffins. Really, I'm not picky. Especially when I have two growing sons who eat more than their dad. Without my mom in town to bake for them, I need all the help I can get."

Debbie nodded in amusement. "How about I check on the muffins for you?"

"I really appreciate it. Thanks."

She entered the kitchen and grabbed an apron from the hook on the wall.

Janet's back was turned. She opened the oven door, peered inside, and moaned. A blast of heat greeted Debbie as she approached her friend. "Greg's here."

Janet pulled out what looked like a pizza covered with rows of caramelized apple slices. She frowned at the golden crust and bubbling sugar before glancing at Debbie. "Yes, he called me yesterday with an order for his crew. But I'm afraid the kuchen is a complete flop. I can't give him this disaster. I feel terrible. Greg and the guys were so excited to try something new, and now I'll disappoint them."

Debbie peered at the pan, trying to discover the flaws. It certainly smelled wonderful. "What's the problem?"

Janet gestured at the crust. "It's too heavy. The dough is ridiculously tough to get right. Too little kneading, and it turns out like a rock. Too much kneading, and it doesn't rise. I think mine is the rock variety. I was in too much of a hurry this morning."

"He said he'd also like some muffins. Do we have any of the blueberry or chocolate chip baked? He said he isn't picky."

Janet grinned. "No, he's not picky. Besides, I don't think Greg is coming solely for the treats."

Cheeks suddenly warm—and not because of the oven—Debbie decided it might be best to ignore the teasing, especially when Greg sat right outside the kitchen. Who knew what he could hear? "Good thing your coffee is exceptional."

Janet laughed and winked at Debbie as she set the kuchen on a wire rack to cool. "The muffins are already in the display case. I'm sure you'll help Greg just fine."

Rolling her eyes at her friend's obvious attempts at matchmaking, Debbie left the kitchen with the coffee carafe and refilled Greg's cup.

"I'm sorry, Greg. Our baker says the kuchen might have the consistency of a hockey puck. But I have plenty of muffins for you and your crew."

Greg stood and carried his coffee to the counter. Again, Debbie was reminded of just how tall he was. And handsome. If she was looking, which she wasn't.

"Muffins would be perfect."

She found two pastry boxes and a pair of plastic gloves. After unfolding the boxes, she picked the biggest and best of the muffins, which was silly, because each one was the picture of perfection, thanks to Janet's flawless technique.

He cleared his throat as he watched her place the muffins side by side. "So what's this I hear about Kim's office?"

When she shot him a glance, he held up a hand with a disarming smile. "Ian, our illustrious police chief, told me. Besides, it's only a matter of time before everyone in Dennison hears the news."

Janet's husband was also Greg's good friend—a fact that made Debbie's social circle remarkably small and well-connected. Sometimes a blessing, sometimes not.

She reached for a blueberry muffin. "Right. Perks of living in a small town. I forget how many people hear through the grapevine, especially after my big-city days. We don't know who entered Kim's office. It's possible the door was left open accidentally and someone was able to slip inside unnoticed."

With Kim and Silas at odds, both blaming each other for the unlocked doors, Debbie didn't know what to think. "Your boys enjoying their summer break?" she asked.

He leaned against the counter as if eager to talk. "They have. I've been warning them that school starts in two weeks. Jaxon is more than ready to start high school. Julian—well, he's a different story. If he had his way, summer would last all year long. I get it. Seventh grade is a tough year."

Debbie chuckled. "No one wants to relive those awkward middle-school years. Mine were marked by way too much hair-spray, bubblegum lip gloss, and tie-dyed shirts." She changed her mind about the contents of the second pastry box and stuffed it with as many sugar cookies drizzled with chocolate icing as she could fit in.

Greg smiled, and his eyes crinkled at the corners. She hastened to add, fully aware of the effect his smile had on her, "Sorry again about the kuchen. We have to keep the customers happy and always coming back, right?"

Greg pulled out his wallet. He really had a pleasant smile and well-trimmed, thick brown hair, despite a stubborn cowlick.

"It's no problem," he said as he handed her a crisp twenty-dollar bill.

Before she could answer, Janet burst into the dining area. She eyed the pastry boxes with an apologetic grimace. "Sorry, Greg. I need more time to figure out the kuchen. Tell the guys I'll hopefully have a sample for them to try pretty soon. If only I had the right recipe. Googling them sometimes proves to be a disaster. I need something old school, tried and true throughout the generations."

Greg tapped his fingers against the counter. "It's German, right? Why not try the people in Sugarcreek? Have you met Cheryl Miller from the Amish gift store, the Swiss Miss? She might help you locate the perfect recipe. The Amish baking in Sugarcreek is fantastic, but it's a little far for those of us in need of a morning sweet fix."

Janet tilted her head as she studied a calendar pinned on the wall. "That's not a bad idea. Maybe Debbie and I can take a quick road trip. It's less than half an hour drive, depending on traffic. I'll call the Swiss Miss as soon as I get a chance."

Of course, if they had an afternoon free for errands, Lapp Lumber would be worth visiting first before driving to the Swiss Miss. They could deal with several tasks in one day and save time.

"I'd love to go," Debbie said. "I've always enjoyed visiting Amish country. I can't imagine a more pleasant afternoon."

Greg looked at her. His mouth parted as if he wanted to say something more and then closed as if he changed his mind.

"Have a wonderful time, ladies." He picked up the boxes and headed for the door. "When you're ready for a taste tester, let me know. I'll gladly do my part. It's a tough job, but someone's gotta do it."

Debbie chuckled and waved goodbye. She headed over to the door and flipped the sign to signal they were open. She froze as she looked through the freshly cleaned glass. There, in the parking lot, waited the exact same Jaguar as the day before.

The last train whistle pierced through the noise of eager children and parents while Frank Sinatra crooned over the speakers. As Debbie wiped a table free of whoopie pie crumbs and smeared icing, she glanced out the café window. Sure enough, the same black car waited in the parking lot. Had it been there all day? Maybe the guy had met someone there and used the property as a carpool parking lot.

The café remained quiet except for an elderly couple sharing a piece of cherry pie topped with melting vanilla ice cream, each taking turns with their spoons. Debbie hid a smile, even though a pang rippled through her. Her fiancé, Reed Brandt, had loved a lattice cherry pie. She sucked in a quick breath and blew it out, the memory still bittersweet despite the years that had passed since his death.

The couple made an adorable picture, and thanks to Annie's hard work, their coffee cups appeared filled. Annie stood by the cash register, adjusting the glass containers filled with old-fashioned candy sticks, including sarsaparilla, orange, blue raspberry, and other flavors for the kids.

"A full day," the young woman murmured as Debbie passed her.

"Wonderfully full," Debbie answered, wiping crumbs from the counter. "We might slow down in the days to come, since the kids will return to school and vacations will end. How about you? Are your college plans settled?"

Annie stopped, her hand hovering above the candy jars. "Mm, hopefully soon. I have a few things to take care of first, some paperwork to fill out, and..." She shrugged.

"Ohio State University, home of the Buckeyes? I thought I heard you mention something about running track for them," Debbie probed.

"Yeah." Annie paused as she replenished the blue raspberry sticks wrapped in cellophane. "It'll be my sophomore year. I'd like to try for liberal arts, maybe a history degree later. But first, I need to see my brother settled into his school year."

Debbie had heard some of Annie's story. Her mom had disappeared years ago, leaving Annie to raise Nicholas. Her father was no help. How tragic for any young woman to be forced to grow up too soon.

"Let me know when you hear. I'm still friends with Abigail Messener. We went to college together. She's a dean for the liberal arts department at Ohio State. I can call her for you this week, if you'd like. Maybe we can help you with the paperwork." She pulled out her phone. "Let me see, I think I have her contact information."

A candy slipped from Annie's grip, cracking as it hit the counter. "Oh no!"

"It's just candy, no worries." Debbie offered a smile. Annie chuckled, but her laughter sounded weak.

Debbie tried to wake up her phone, but the battery had run out. She handed the wet cloth to Annie and untied her apron. "Do you mind watching the register while I duck out for a moment? I have a charger in my car, and I'd like to take a short walk."

Annie took the cloth and apron. "Not at all. Janet's in the kitchen taking a break. I'm sure between the two of us, we'll manage."

Debbie headed outside, enjoying the August warmth sweltering from the pavement. She walked past the museum housed within the train station and the static train cars designated as special displays, including a 1920s Pullman sleeper car, newly opened as a bed and breakfast for those determined to experience the train station to the fullest extent possible. The only cars currently closed for August, because of renovations, were the hospital car, which was painted a deep burgundy with black trim, and a second Pullman car, purchased because of the success of the first. A series of ropes prevented tourists from entering the cars, although workers had continually rotated in and out, armed with supplies.

Thankfully, the tourists had thinned somewhat as Debbie strolled along the sidewalk. She enjoyed seeing the families with sleeping toddlers in strollers wandering about the grounds. Kids milled with parents, equally fascinated with the displays.

On the main platform, the well-dressed stranger sat on a bench while children ran past with helium balloons tied to their wrists. She stepped to the left, closer to the multipaned windows of the station and out of his peripheral vision. He glanced at his watch and sighed. If he was waiting for someone, surely, he must be getting anxious. With pressed trousers and an expensive white collared shirt, he didn't appear as though he was on vacation.

He pulled out his phone and scrolled, biting his bottom lip as he stared at the device. Yesterday and today, he had visited the station. Alone. Debbie was about to walk back to the café when she heard tapping on the window behind her. She turned and saw Kim beckoning to her.

"Debbie, just the woman I want to see," Kim called when Debbie entered the train museum. Kim marched across the floor toward her with a clipboard pinned beneath her arm. "I've been wanting to chat with you all day, but I couldn't get away from my desk."

Debbie shoved her hands into her pockets. "Any more issues with the missing items?"

Kim pursed her lips. "No. But I wanted you and Janet to know that I'm installing additional video cameras around the premises. The security company should have everything taken care of within a couple of weeks, or sooner, hopefully. I don't want to see anything else taken."

"What a great idea. At least the displays were untouched."

Kim shifted her clipboard. "I'm thankful about that. I called Ian to come over and check everything out, and he couldn't find any signs of a break-in. What more can I do?"

Debbie glanced at the large window with a view of the platform, remembering her grandmother's tray. She really needed to tell her mom about it, but she had hoped the tray would turn up sooner rather than later. She turned her attention to the train platform. "Have you noticed that man on the bench out there? He's been here the last two days, and he seems to be waiting for someone or something."

Kim leaned forward, following Debbie's line of vision. Her eyebrows rose as she studied the man. "That's the same man who had quite a few questions about my mom's items in the stationmaster display case. He asked if he could go through her record book in the museum section. I refused, of course. Only university historians get access to encased items. I can't have greasy fingerprints ruining fragile paper."

"Did he mention his name?"

Kim pressed a finger against her lips, pondering the question. "I believe so. Rick? Rich? Let me check the guest book and see if he signed it." Debbie followed Kim to a small table against the wall next to a display case containing a standard World War II uniform. She waited as Debbie flipped through the pages lined with signatures of every style.

"Aha!" Kim smiled as she pointed to a bold signature. "Richard Brown." She flipped the pages of the guest book to the blank page and realigned the pen. "Once I get all the cameras working, we should be able to spot whoever tries to steal from the station again."

"Keep me posted, will you?" Debbie headed to the exit. As she pushed on the brass door handle, she saw the stranger leave the platform, his brows pulled down as he angled through the dwindling crowd. She veered to the left, toward her car, to retrieve her phone charger.

A couple of minutes later, on her way back to the café, Debbie saw that the stranger had stopped near one of the stationary railcar displays. After looking over his shoulder, he reached into his pocket, withdrew something, and then placed it next to the nearby lamppost.

She watched with wonder as he suddenly pivoted and ran to his car then slid in quickly and slammed the door behind him. The car revved to life and backed out, giving her a glimpse of his stern profile as he passed. When she reached the lamppost, a small envelope lay facedown on the pavement. The paper was soft, yellowed with age. Debbie flipped it over, scanning the faded brown script.

The address made her gasp.

*Eileen Turner*
*329 Spring Road*
*Dennison, OH 44621*

No stamp or return address. She touched the sealed part of the envelope, still snug as could be. What was inside that envelope and, perhaps more importantly, why did Richard Brown leave it by the lamppost?

# CHAPTER SIX

*D*ebbie passed the envelope to Kim, who angled it in such a way that Janet could read it at the same time.

"I'd love to know what's inside," Janet murmured. She still wore her striped apron and had left Annie in charge of the cash register once Debbie barged into the café with the envelope. The women stood in the kitchen.

"Do you think I should open it?" Kim asked. "Honestly, I hate the idea of reading my mother's mail without her seeing it first. But I've been handling all of her correspondence since she moved into Good Shepherd."

"It might not hurt to check," Debbie said. "We don't know who this man is or what he wants with your mom to deliver a letter in such a clandestine manner."

Janet wrinkled her nose. "It's almost as if he didn't want Eileen to get it. Honestly, the post office is just a few blocks away. He could have taken it there. Why leave it at the lamppost?"

"Right," Debbie agreed. "We know he asked Kim plenty of questions about Eileen's work as the stationmaster." She turned to Kim. "Did you tell him she's your mother?"

Kim shook her head. "I didn't. Once in a while I'll tell people I'm the stationmaster's daughter, and, of course, all the longtime residents know." She chewed her lip as she fingered the sealed portion of the envelope. "This seems very old. It reminds me of the historical letters we have displayed in the museum."

"An old letter?" Annie had come into the kitchen and now stood on tiptoes to see over Janet's shoulder. "Just how old?"

"Considering someone addressed it to Eileen Turner, which is my mother's maiden name, I'm guessing it's from the thirties or forties," Kim answered.

"I love anything historical," Annie gushed as she pushed her way into the group, forcing Kim to step backward. "Can I see?"

Debbie pressed her lips together to prevent herself from curbing Annie's enthusiasm. It wasn't every day someone dropped off something mysterious at the station. Could she really blame Annie for being curious?

"It belongs to your mom," Debbie said. "Maybe you should call her and ask for permission to open it."

Kim brightened. "I'll call her right now."

Debbie followed her friends to Kim's office. Annie traipsed close enough to step on the back of Debbie's heel.

"Ouch," Debbie yelped, rubbing the spot.

Annie came to an abrupt stop. "I'm so sorry. I didn't mean to step on you," she said.

"Annie, you need to go back to the café," Debbie said. "We can't all be gone at the same time."

Annie looked so disappointed, Debbie almost volunteered to be the one to watch the café. But then the young woman smiled. "Okay," she said. "But if it's something exciting, I wanna know."

Somehow, it felt fitting to call Eileen from her old office. Oak bookshelves lined the plastered walls. A framed tinted photo of Eileen hung between two of them, her cheeks faintly blushing thanks to a skilled artist. Despite the neat interior, Kim's desk was strewn with potential advertisements for the Christmas holidays. A box of donated items waiting to be cataloged sat on a separate table.

Kim snatched her cell phone from her desk and tapped in the number. "Hi Mom. You'll never believe what just happened. A man left an envelope addressed to you here at the station. Would you like me to open it and read it to you? Or I can stop by with it later and let you read it. Oh—who's winning?" She laughed. "You tell Ray that we all say hello."

Kim smiled and winked at Debbie. Debbie chuckled under her breath. Ray Zink and Eileen were close friends and now practically neighbors.

"All right then. I'll let you go and win that game. Yes, I'll bring the envelope when I come by tonight." Kim ended the call. "Mom says we can open it. Apparently, I called at the wrong time. She and Ray are playing bingo."

"Winning bingo is important," Janet said. "I'm amazed at how competitive the residents are with each other."

"I can't deny that I'm curious to see what's inside." Kim reached for a pearl-handled letter opener. She carefully slit the envelope, pulled out a thin sheaf of paper, and unfolded it. "It's dated March 18, 1945." She began to read. "'Dear Eileen, thank you for your letters. You have sent me a taste of home. My family still refuses to answer me, and if it was not for you, I would have no idea what happens in Dennison. I will forever be grateful for you and the books you gave me just before I left for training. Forgive me for my recent silence since my platoon shipped to Luzon, an island in the Philippines, thanks to General MacArthur's latest orders.'"

Kim pulled back from the paper, squinting. "I'm shocked censors didn't remove this information."

"I don't think it was ever sent," Debbie said as she leaned forward to study the faint script. Usually, such letters contained blotted-out sections hiding important information. "For two reasons. One, because there's no postmark, and two, because you're right. No censor would allow such a specific location."

Kim resumed reading. "'However, I fear this may be the last letter I send, and certainly the hardest one I'll ever write. Eileen, I want you to be free. I'm not the same man who listened to Vera Lynn with you at the Revco Drugstore. The war has changed me. You deserve so much more than I can offer. Marry a man who will dance to 'We'll Meet Again' with you and sweep you off your feet. Yours truly, Samuel.'"

A silence fell, with only the sound of the silver wall clock ticking steadily. Outside the station window, the shriek of the train whistle broke the shock.

"Wow." Debbie swallowed. "A Dear Jane letter. Who was Samuel?"

Kim studied the letter, her brow pinched. "I don't know. Dad would have never sent something like this to Mom. I remember him twirling her in the kitchen to Frank Sinatra. He was so in love with her, even until the very end when he was in hospice. I always believed she loved only him. I've never heard of this man."

Janet said gently, "Yet it appears as though she knew him well enough to have some sort of engagement or understanding with him."

Kim's frown deepened. "Mom never mentioned him to me. Not once. I've been helping her compile her scrapbooks. We just went through some of her old photos a few weeks ago. If there was a picture of this Samuel guy, she never said anything. I wonder what happened to him. And I wonder if Mom will be glad to get this letter."

The room, despite the towering fourteen-foot ceilings, suddenly felt immeasurably small. Debbie's voice thickened as memories of Reed crowded her thoughts. "Closure can be a gift. Everyone needs some form of it."

She didn't feel like explaining any further, but the compassionate look Janet shot her spoke volumes. Hadn't she waited for word regarding Reed following his last mission in Afghanistan? How painful the wait proved as days stretched into weeks and months until, at last, a dreadful phone call. He had been held hostage and later killed. She couldn't imagine not knowing a loved one's fate and somehow finding the courage to move forward.

But this was Eileen's loss to deal with, and not hers.

Kim carefully placed the letter back into the envelope. "Why did Mom keep Samuel a secret all these years?"

# CHAPTER SEVEN

Eileen rested on a love seat in the Good Shepherd common area. Framed by a pool of sunshine, she wore a purple pantsuit and a long gold chain with an oval locket. Her white hair remained perfectly curled, and her smidgen of tasteful blush and lipstick made Debbie smile.

Kim, however, appeared flustered. She leaned over her mother to kiss her papery cheek. "You look fabulous as always, Mom. I hope you don't mind, but I brought some friends to see you this afternoon. How was bingo?"

"We had fun. Ray won this time." Eileen waved a blue-veined hand, gesturing to the nearby burgundy wingbacks beside a fake tree tilting precariously in a wicker pot. Dated brass lamps with frosted shades perched on oak tables, reminding Debbie of her grandmother's living room. All that was missing was a crocheted doily.

Eileen beamed at Debbie. "I always love seeing you and Janet. You really should visit more often. I hear the cooks are serving lasagna tonight. I'd be happy to share."

Lasagna sounded good. Debbie had eaten half a muffin for lunch. After locking the café and saying goodbye to a lingering Annie— firmly but gently—Debbie wanted nothing more than to relax at home with a good supper. But first, the letter and Eileen.

Janet held up a small box and lifted the lid to reveal the contents. "I brought you some whoopie pies for dessert. Made by our very own Debbie."

"Goodness." Eileen reached for the box. "Those look scrumptious."

As Debbie and the others settled next to Eileen, Kim cleared her throat. "Mom, our visit isn't simply to drop off dessert. Like I told you on the phone, a man brought an envelope to the train station. He came in yesterday and asked about the stationmaster displays, including yours. He wanted to see your logbooks and a sample of your writing. I refused, of course. But then today Debbie saw him put this next to one of the lampposts. His name is Richard Brown. Does that name sound familiar to you?"

Kim reached into her purse, withdrew the envelope, and handed it to Eileen.

"Richard Brown? Doesn't sound familiar, but it's possible I'm forgetting something at my age." The smile on Eileen's face dimmed as she took the paper out of the envelope. With a trembling hand, she pushed her glasses up the bridge of her nose and quietly read the contents. A shudder rippled across her frail shoulders, and she dropped the letter to her lap. She pressed a hand against her mouth and murmured, "Oh, Samuel."

Kim found a tissue in her purse and handed it to her mother. "Who is Samuel, Mom? Did Dad know about him?"

Eileen dabbed at the corners of her eyes and then crumpled the tissue into a ball in her fist. "Oh, honey, let me explain. Before I knew your father, I met another man in town. I thought I loved Samuel and he loved me, but in the end, he disappeared."

Debbie leaned forward, reaching a hand to cover Eileen's. The older woman's fingers trembled beneath Debbie's grip. "I'm so sorry you were hurt. How hard this must be for you. Did you ever hear from Samuel when he fought overseas?"

Eileen sighed. "Only a few letters. My last memory is of him climbing onto the train and waving goodbye to me. He never returned to his family or his business, Lapp Lumber. I prayed for him for years, hoping he survived the war."

Goose bumps skittered across Debbie's arms as the name slowly registered. "Wait. Lapp Lumber? As in Daniel Lapp's lumberyard?"

"Yes. Elijah Lapp had always intended the lumberyard to pass to Samuel. But Samuel didn't want that for his life. He was so different from his brother, Jacob. Samuel wanted nothing more than to find a remote hill and read until sunset. Daniel is Jacob's son."

"Mom, you fell in love with an Amish man who went to war?" Kim's voice raised a few notches, startling an aide who balanced a tray with plastic cups of orange juice.

"Yes, I fell in love with him. We first met when he was nineteen and I was twenty, during his rumspringa, and we just had such a strong connection, we kept seeing each other over the next few years. Quietly, of course. Your grandfather didn't approve one bit. Nor did Samuel's father. When I covered the ticket booth before being promoted to stationmaster, we would meet once a week for lunch or dinner, or whenever he could get away from work. However, as the war picked up and soldiers came from all corners of the United States, he couldn't bear to stay home and watch. Then one day he decided he was going away to do his part. After the war ended, I waited and waited, hoping to see him. It was as if he had vanished without a trace. His family refused to speak with me. For years, I worried about him. Was he suffering as a prisoner of war or had he died alone in some forgotten field in France?"

Kim blew out a breath, and Eileen dabbed at a tear trickling down her cheek. How long had she held on to this secret, grieving in silence, while wondering what had happened to her first love?

Debbie patted Eileen's arm. "We need to replace some wainscoting in the café and are going to visit Daniel's business tomorrow afternoon. Is there any chance anyone there might know what happened to Samuel?"

Eileen's shoulders slumped, her voice warbling and soft. "If the Lapp family knew anything, they never told me. In fact, they let me know years ago that I'm not welcome to step foot into Lapp Lumber."

# CHAPTER EIGHT

*Dennison, Ohio*
*May 1943*

*Eileen sucked in a sharp breath as she studied the stranger in front of her. It was amazing what a haircut and a tailored suit could do to a man. The demeanor of her gentle Samuel had hardened overnight, his jaw sharper and leaner than she remembered. Without the soft golden curls around his neck and forehead and the weathered blue cotton shirts and loose-fitting pants, he exuded something she couldn't quite define. Or like. The fitted brown coat clung to his broad shoulders. His hat shadowed his blue eyes. She took in the rest of his appearance, her throat squeezing tight. Neatly pressed pants. Shoes shined bright enough to reflect the lights swinging above her.*

*"I can't believe you're leaving," she finally said. Behind her, soldiers swarmed into the railcars, their*

laughter and jovial goodbyes masking the seriousness of their journey.

Samuel stepped closer, raising her chin with a finger. "You know I have to go. It's my duty."

Moisture welled in her eyes, and before she could gain control, a traitorous tear slid down her cheek. How well she knew duty, especially her own to Papa and the weight of working to support them both pressing on her thoughts every single day. While she remained at the station, so many childhood friends left Dennison, many likely never to return. And now Samuel, who was supposed to be her rock, would leave on a similar train in a few minutes. Was it selfish for her to cry, to feel so alone already?

Before she could answer, he kissed her right in front of everyone. A few nearby soldiers whistled their approval. When Samuel pulled back, she saw a sheen gather in his eyes as well.

"I'll come back for you, liebling, I promise. I've packed the books you gave me. I will read them, thinking of my Eileen. As soon as I can, I'll write. We'll meet again, I promise."

Overwhelmed, she tugged his head down for one more kiss. The train whistle pierced through her, shrill and insistent, demanding he leave immediately. She followed him to the platform swarming with soldiers and newly enlisted men.

*Reluctantly, Samuel pulled away from her, reaching to grab his worn suitcase with the loose handle. With a lopsided grin, he boarded the train that was packed with young men from as far away as Texas and California. They stuck their heads out the open windows, waving at the pretty girls lined up in a row holding sandwich and doughnut trays.*

*The train screeched again, and the engine puffed and chuffed, the wheels rolling forward, carrying him away from her. She remained planted on the platform, her limbs heavy, as his handsome face disappeared from view. A sob threatened to bubble up within her, but she quelled it as she sidestepped family members gathered in clusters to say goodbye to their sons, grandsons, husbands, and brothers.*

*One person caught her attention, standing out in a sea of brown and khaki uniforms, wearing familiar navy pants and suspenders and a wrinkled blue shirt. Her heart came to a shuddering halt as she stared at the tall teenager who turned around to glare at her. Jacob Lapp. As he yanked his straw hat lower, he mouthed something hateful. Despite the low roar of the train station, she heard a word that made her stomach roil.*

Jezebel.

# CHAPTER NINE

On Wednesday afternoon Debbie rode with Janet to Lapp Lumber. It was located outside Dennison, southeast of the Uhrichsville community. Debbie climbed out of the car, pulling off her enormous black sunglasses to scan the storefront. Tension pooled in her shoulders as she studied the grounds. She gritted her teeth, certain she wouldn't like the Lapp men, considering all she had heard. Despite her misgivings, the tall red building appeared well-kept, the metal roof reflecting the blistering August sun with a blinding glare. A pair of cheerful red pots bloomed with pink geraniums at the front entrance. Behind the main building, a large yard full of lumber suggested a thriving business.

She checked her watch. Nearly three o'clock. "I hope we aren't too late."

"We've got over an hour before we visit the Swiss Miss in Sugarcreek. Cheryl said she would wait for us," Janet assured her as she shut the car door with a thud.

Debbie led the way to the front door, her pulse picking up a notch as she remembered Eileen's tearful confession and Becky's financial woes. What kind of business banned a beloved town icon from the premises and refused to honor a professional agreement?

As she and Janet entered the building, an overhead brass bell jingled a merry tune. A young woman wearing a simple blue dress, white apron, and a pleated prayer *kapp* covering wispy blond hair sat behind a counter, carefully writing in a spiral notebook. She raised her head to see Debbie, her voice disarmingly soft and warm. "Good afternoon, and *willkumme.*"

"Hi." Debbie smiled as she reached the counter. "I'm Debbie Albright. I'm hoping you can help me. My partner, Janet Shaw, and I operate the Whistle Stop Café at the train station. We need some of the historic wainscoting replaced."

Might as well start with the good news before bringing up the letter.

The young woman rose from her stool. "Do you have a sample? I am sure my daed could help."

"Are you Daniel Lapp's daughter?" Debbie asked, intrigued by the younger woman's sweet demeanor, which was at odds with what she had heard about Lapp Lumber.

"Ja, I am the youngest. I am Hannah."

Janet reached into her bag and produced a picture of the trim. "It has to be exact, especially since the train station is now considered a historic site and a registered landmark. Any renovation has to match the original as perfectly as possible. I understand it's called Blackthorn trim."

Hannah took the picture and examined it. "*Wunderbaar.* How much do you need?"

As Janet gave the measurements, Debbie caught a glimpse of blue moving at the back of the store. A young man dressed in work pants, suspenders, and a blue button-down shirt watched closely. He offered no smile, unlike Hannah.

"What do you think, Debbie? Should we order additional bead-board as a precaution?" Janet's question drew Debbie's attention back to the project. She noticed a stunning curio cabinet of light oak against the wall. The simple lines would be perfect for the café, offering a place for the antique kitchen utensils to be displayed for customers. She still held out hope that her grandmother's tray would return soon.

"I think we could order an extra panel or two. May I ask who made that beautiful cabinet?" Debbie asked.

Hannah's gaze slid to the cabinet. "My daed or *bruder* could make one custom for you. We also have several other pieces to take home today, including this cabinet. It is three fifty."

Three hundred and fifty dollars. Not a bad price, and tempting, considering the beauty of the piece. A rich, varnished sheen brought out the grain of the wood.

"Worth every penny, I'm sure. Sadly, I'll have to wait on it, but one day I'd love to place an order." Debbie couldn't help but feel for Hannah, especially with the conversation coming next.

*Lord, Janet and I could really use some wisdom in this situation. Please help us find closure for Eileen.*

"Actually, we aren't here solely for trim. We received a letter that ought to be discussed with your father. Could we speak to him? It's a letter from World War II, written by one of your relatives."

Hannah frowned. "A letter from family?"

Debbie's stomach clenched at the thought that she was causing distress, and she softened her tone. "Yes, from Samuel Lapp. I understand he was the son of Elijah Lapp. Someone dropped the letter at the train station. Samuel addressed it to Eileen Turner. I realize many years have passed, but she would like to know what happened to her old friend. Is there anything you can tell me about Samuel?"

"Hannah!" The young man approached the counter, his tone sharp. "I will handle this."

Hannah frowned again, her forehead crinkling with dismay. Eyes downcast, she placed her pen on the counter and left, but not before glancing over her shoulder, her expression worried.

"We do not discuss our family affairs with customers. If you have an order, I can help. Otherwise, I will ask you to leave immediately." The man splayed his fingers on the counter. His brusque manner jarred Debbie.

Seemingly nonplussed, Janet pushed her sunglasses onto her head. "We'd like to finish our order for trim and beadboard. Just a small amount to repair a space about three feet by five feet. Can you give us an estimate?"

He muttered an amount then filled out an order form. He tore the yellow copy from the pad and slid it over to Debbie. She reached into her purse, bypassing the credit cards to pull out cash.

His mouth pinched white, as if doing business with Debbie proved distasteful. "You do not need it today, do you? I have a few other orders to finish this afternoon before I can cut the wood and beadboard."

As much as she wanted to avoid offending the sullen young man, she shook her head. "I'd prefer not to make a second trip, if possible."

He grunted in response.

Janet tried a little sweetness. "Actually, maybe you can help us with another matter as well. We're hunting for a traditional kuchen recipe. Would you know of anyone who might be interested in sharing?"

His tense posture relaxed somewhat. "You will probably find Sugarcreek as good as any place for baking. If you'll excuse me—"

He abruptly pivoted on his heel and left Debbie and Janet at the counter.

"Good thing we didn't bring up Becky's lost furniture order," Janet said.

Debbie bit back her exasperation, her frustration mounting by the minute. "No kidding. I almost bought the cabinet but then thought better of it, knowing Becky hasn't received her furniture from the Lapps yet. She said she wasn't treated very well either. I'd hate to pay for something and not receive it. At least our trip won't be a total loss if we get the trim and a recipe."

How disappointing and very curious to witness the young man's reaction to Eileen's name. She didn't deserve such harsh treatment.

A cough came from behind a shelf that housed an assortment of nails, screws, and other building supplies. Hannah peeked around it, her eyes wide. A sheepish smile crossed her face as she hurried over to them.

"I have several kuchen recipes," she whispered. "I would be happy to share them with you. They are back at the house, but if you leave an address, I will mail them to you as soon as I can." She pushed the order pad and the pen toward Janet. "Please do not mind my bruder, Benjamin. He is—he is a little flustered these days. He has had a hard week."

Janet wrote her home address and then asked a couple of questions regarding techniques for achieving the lightest possible dough. Hannah appeared all too happy to answer.

She leaned closer to Debbie, dropping her voice to a whisper. "I overheard your conversation about your friend's order being unfulfilled. Forgive me for eavesdropping. I will check into your friend

Becky's furniture order, ja? I am sure it is a simple misunderstanding on my daed's part. We don't want anyone to feel cheated. My *maam* taught me differently."

Debbie smiled. "Bless you, Hannah. I know Becky will really appreciate that. She'll be grateful for any help you can provide."

"How long has Lapp Lumber existed?" Janet asked, sitting down on the bench next to the counter.

"My great-grandfather, Elijah Lapp, did not have enough land to farm, so he made furniture and cut lumber. Eventually his son, Jacob, took over, and now my daed and Benjamin run the business."

"Any other family members in the business?" Janet probed, echoing Debbie's thoughts.

Hannah hesitated for the briefest moment. "Only my daed inherited Lapp Lumber." A shadow crossed her face, as if she might have said too much. The doorbell jingled a second time, and another customer entered. His long beard, tinged with gray, and his clothing so similar to Benjamin's, marked him as Amish.

"Hannah Lapp, just the one I wanted to see," the older man boomed with good humor as the door swung closed behind him.

"I am sorry, I must help this customer." Eyes yet again downcast, Hannah bustled around the counter to greet the newcomer, leaving Debbie and Janet alone.

If Hannah hadn't been interrupted, what else might she have shared?

# CHAPTER TEN

*D*riving into Sugarcreek brought pure nostalgic joy. Only nineteen miles northwest of Dennison, Sugarcreek offered a different vista—a peaceful Amish life with the flavor of Swiss culture. Debbie peered out the car window as Janet eased into a parking spot in front of a charming store painted a creamy white with cornflower-blue accents and red shutters. Amish gifts lined the old-fashioned storefront windows, including a collection of faceless dolls wearing plain dresses layered with pristine aprons. Handmade wooden toys, including a horse with a braided tail and even a miniature train, brought a whimsical charm to the display.

"Delightful, isn't it?" Janet smiled as she turned off the engine and took in the surroundings.

"It's been years since I've visited Sugarcreek. Brings back wonderful memories. Don't you dare let me leave without buying jam for my mom. She'll never forgive me if I don't bring her a gift." Perhaps a gift for her mother would soothe the bad news about the missing family tray. She would have to call her soon and let her know. Especially now that she had waited two days since learning of its disappearance and there was still no sign of it.

Inside the store, Debbie heaved a sigh of relief. Here, she felt immediately welcomed and safe. So different from the difficult visit to Lapp Lumber. After a thirty-five-minute wait and no goods loaded into the car, Debbie and Janet had no choice but to abandon the lumberyard in order to catch Cheryl before closing time.

Artfully decorated shelves housed Amish goods, including handmade soaps, candles, and candies. Colorful quilts in every hue possible lay on wooden racks. Debbie wandered to one quilt with a purple star pattern. She marveled at the precise, tiny stitches marching in a neat row and imagined where this quilt would fit in her home. But one look at the price tag plummeted any hopes of purchase. She didn't have twelve hundred dollars to spare. Not after the renovations to her house and the café. Her gut clenched at the reality of mounting expenses.

"Is that you, Janet?" a woman called from the back of the store. She emerged through the curtains that hung over a doorway, her slim jeans and tunic top at odds with the traditional Amish goods and decor.

"Cheryl!" Janet exclaimed. "Thank you so much for helping us. I'm so excited to try your mother-in-law's recipes. Would you believe Hannah Lapp has already promised me the same?"

"Hannah is a sweetheart and a wonderful baker." Cheryl chuckled as she held out a green folder for Janet. "Naomi wants to say hello, but she's doling out snacks to Rebecca and Matthew. They'll all be out soon."

After introductions, Janet shared about the experience at Lapp Lumber. "I've never seen someone so put out to discover we work at the Dennison depot."

Debbie folded her arms across her chest, her mind flashing to Benjamin's sneer when he took the order. "Hannah said her brother had a hard week. It's a shame he isn't more like his sister."

Cheryl nodded, her expression neutral. "The Lapps have been part of the community for a long time and are well known in the area."

Debbie changed the subject. "We also wondered if you could help us locate an Amish man named Samuel Lapp, who fought during World War II."

Cheryl's eyes sparkled with mischief. "Sounds intriguing. Naomi and I love a good mystery. Let's ask her if she knows anything."

The curtains parted again, and a middle-aged Amish woman entered holding a young boy's hand while a girl followed close behind, her hair in twin braids.

Naomi's deep blue dress and apron were of the traditional Amish style, and her brown hair was all but hidden beneath a pleated kapp. The little boy ducked behind his grandmother as Cheryl reached for her daughter. "This is Rebecca, my oldest. She's six years old, and she's going to start school in the fall. Tell the ladies how old you are, Matthew."

He shook his head.

Rebecca didn't share her brother's shyness. "He's four." She held up four fingers with a smile. "He could show you himself, but *Grossmammi* gave him a half-moon pie, and I bet his hands are sticky."

Debbie smiled. "Half-moon pies are some of my favorite treats."

Janet had first made the handheld flaky pastry last month, stuffing the pies with fragrant cinnamon and apple slices. The dessert had proved a hit, along with the original recipe for the Salvation Army doughnuts.

Naomi beamed as she patted her grandson's shoulder. "Matthew and Rebecca are learning to bake with me, aren't you, lieblings?" She turned to Debbie. "You mentioned the Lapps?"

Debbie nodded. "Yes. It's quite a story. Samuel Lapp fell in love with Eileen Turner, now Palmer, who ran the train station during the war. He volunteered to fight and never returned. She eventually married and had a daughter, Kim, who currently oversees the museum. A visitor dropped off a letter for Eileen the other day, and lo and behold—Samuel Lapp wrote it years ago. Eileen had always wondered what happened to him. We hoped you could help us discover his whereabouts."

Naomi frowned as Matthew let go of her hand to dash toward a wooden horse. "Samuel Lapp of Lapp Lumber. Yes, I remember hearing about some of our plain folk enlisting."

"The Lapps refused to answer my questions about him. I understand they even barred Eileen from entering the lumberyard."

"Contact with certain Englischers can be regulated, depending on the bishop of the area. I am sure the parents might have worried over their son's decision to date Eileen, but such fear does not condone their actions," Naomi said as her granddaughter replaced Matthew's spot to snuggle close.

Cheryl smiled at her mother-in-law. "Levi and I are so blessed to be close to you and Seth. I can't imagine living with a family so torn apart."

Naomi nodded as she smoothed Rebecca's hair. "Ja, families need each other."

Debbie mulled over the information. "Was Samuel shunned?"

Naomi's expression saddened. "Oh yes, I am certain of it. According to the *Ordnung*, Samuel abandoned his faith when he dated an Englischer and enlisted to fight. The Amish were, and still are, considered conscientious objectors, similar to the stricter

Mennonite and Quaker groups. However, your Samuel would not be the first conscientious objector to do such a thing. Cheryl can share what she knows from another man who went to war as a medic. He sent home the money he earned, and the family stored it in the walls of a cottage in Sugarcreek."

Cheryl sighed as she reached for her son, who, by now, had plucked a candy bar from the nearest shelf. "Frank Raber's mother and stepfather also abandoned him when he left for the war. Later, Frank became a physician, drawing from his experience as a medic in the Pacific. He never returned to the Sugarcreek area. If we hadn't renovated the cottages to house abused women, we might never have discovered Frank's story. You should not give up trying to discover the truth of Samuel's story."

Debbie made a mental note of the name, excitement trilling through her veins. "Is it possible the men knew each other? Could one have influenced the other?"

Cheryl looked at Naomi. "I wonder if Frank spoke with Samuel Lapp and encouraged him to leave the Amish community." She turned to Debbie and Janet. "I'll call Frank's daughter, Linda, and see if she knows anything."

Later that evening, Debbie glanced at the clock in her kitchen. The gilt arms pointed to six forty-five. The perfect time to call her mother about the tray.

Her mother answered immediately. "Sweetheart, how is everything?"

Debbie rubbed her forehead. "Hi, Mom. I just wanted to let you know that some items went missing from Kim's office the other day, including Grandma's tray. So far, we've seen no sign of it."

Her mother remained silent.

"Apparently the tray was worth more than we realized. Kim thinks it would sell for three hundred dollars or more," Debbie said.

"For that old thing? I'm shocked."

"I think the value to our family is more sentimental. A few items related to the Salvation Army kitchen also went missing."

"Hopefully things will turn up soon," her mother said. "I don't know how Kim manages to keep everything working so smoothly. I wouldn't blame her if an item or two got misplaced."

Was that all it was? A simple mistake? Kim didn't seem to think so. Debbie wasn't so certain either.

"I'll let you know if and when the tray turns up again. I'm sorry."

"Your grandmother would be so proud of you opening the café. I just wanted a little bit of her to inspire you. Don't let this get you down."

Debbie sighed as she ended the phone call. Of course, her mother would hear the frustration in her daughter's voice and offer encouragement. And it worked. Debbie felt a new confidence that, one way or another, she'd get down to the bottom of the missing items in the museum and Eileen's letter from Samuel. So much history lay within the station. So many threads. It certainly wouldn't hurt to recruit a little help, would it?

Should she call Greg on a Wednesday evening, or would he still be working? Hopefully he had finished supper at his house and it would be safe to call. He had proven so helpful in the past whenever she had questions about the history of Dennison, especially since he knew practically everyone in town. Like Kim, Greg loved history.

She pulled her cell phone closer to her and stared at the dark screen for a moment or two before finally swiping to find his number. Oh, goodness. Why did she feel like she'd swallowed a jar full of dragonflies? She wasn't asking him to escort her to homecoming or go out on a date.

"Hello?"

"Hi, Greg, it's Debbie." She paused.

"Debbie," he exclaimed, as if surprised. "Good to hear from you. Tell Janet the muffins were a huge hit with my guys."

"Janet will be thrilled. I hope I'm not calling too late. It's just that I had a few questions for you regarding a situation."

The phone remained silent for a few beats. "A situation? Is everything okay at the train station, or did more things go missing?"

His protective tone made her smile. "No, no more missing antiques. I'm wondering if you might help me track down a missing member of the community."

"Oh?"

Debbie filled Greg in on the letter and her reception at Lapp Lumber. "It's clear we won't get the answers we need from Daniel. Is there any way you can help me discover what happened to Samuel Lapp? Cheryl from the Swiss Miss in Sugarcreek is on it as well, but I figured I could use additional insight."

An exuberant shout in the background came from Greg's side. The phone rustled as if being muffled by a hand, and then his voice resonated clearly. "I'd like to help. It's just that the boys have a special game night at the church in fifteen minutes, and I volunteered to supervise dodgeball in the gym."

Her cheeks heated with embarrassment. How silly of her to assume Greg would be free. And how wonderful that he spent his night in such a way.

"I'm so sorry—I didn't mean to interrupt your plans."

"No, no. It's fine," he said. "Why don't we talk about it over lunch on Sunday? I need to take the boys somewhere right after church, but I can meet you at Buona Vita. Say one thirty?"

"Great, looking forward to it," she said before ending the call. This wasn't a date. Just friends helping friends, and if there was anything Greg did well, it was watching over his community. As president of the local chamber of commerce, he knew more about Dennison, Ohio, than anyone else.

Blowing out a harsh breath, she retrieved her laptop. Her Wednesday night might not be as exciting as Greg's, but she had some research to do about the mysterious visitor who had discarded the letter. Finding a comfortable spot on the sofa, she opened her computer. Her fingers flew across the keys as she typed *Richard Brown*. A quick search revealed nothing of interest. Faces popped up in the search, including a young and overly tanned plastic surgeon in Austin, Texas, but no one resembled the sandy-haired man she had observed at the train station.

Before Debbie realized how long her search had taken, minutes slid into an hour and then longer when she added more searches. *Frank Raber. Samuel Lapp.* Not much chance of an Amish man leaving a mark on the internet, but would he at least have an obituary? *Luzon. Censorship of wartime mail.* And then, just because she wanted to know for herself, *1940 Southern Dairies Sealtest Ice Cream tray.*

Debbie rubbed her aching eyes and glanced at the time. Ten o'clock, and she was still no closer to an answer. Somehow, Richard was the key to finding a missing soldier. But how could she find him when there were far too many Richard Browns in the world?

# CHAPTER ELEVEN

*S*aturday proved to be another busy day at the café. Debbie had just finished refilling the coffee maker when she caught a glimpse of black flashing past the windows. Then she saw a horse and buggy shudder to a halt right outside the front door. A young mother and her three children sitting in a booth craned their necks to see out the windows, their morning breakfast of orange-glazed scones and muffins forgotten. The mother slipped her hand into her purse and pulled out her phone, saying something about taking a picture.

"I think we have company," Annie said.

Debbie added water to the coffee machine even though her curiosity nearly drove her to the nearest window. Silently, she urged the young mother to return the phone to her bag. The Amish didn't like their pictures taken without permission. She glimpsed the same sullen young Amish man from Lapp Lumber who had nearly chased her from the store. He waited by the horses while another man climbed down and opened the café door.

Without being told, Debbie knew the man was Daniel Lapp. His full beard covered his lower jaw, the dull blond hue weathered with streaks of gray. She paused, remembering her last visit with Benjamin Lapp. He had left her and Janet waiting over half an hour before they eventually had to leave. Not a positive first impression for new customers. Becky's complaint made all the more sense.

Daniel entered the café and scanned the room before settling on her, choosing to ignore the gawking mother and her children.

"Are you Debbie Albright, the owner here?" His voice deepened as he marched toward the glass display of treats.

Debbie squared her shoulders, keeping her expression neutral since she was aware of customers watching the exchange. "Half owner. Janet Shaw is my partner."

Daniel reached the counter, his blue-eyed gaze sharpening. "I understand an apology is in order. My son was rude to you and did not offer timely service. That is not our way."

Of all the scenarios playing out in her mind of meeting Daniel Lapp, this was not one of them. Speechless, Debbie could only stare at him and hope she wasn't gaping like a fish out of water.

"I wanted you to know that I have brought your millwork and beadboard as a peace offering. I would like you to consider it a gift and hope you will use Lapp Lumber in the future."

"I—thank you." Debbie struggled to get the words out. "But really, I must insist on paying."

He shook his head. "*Ne*. My *dochder*, Hannah, told me the story of your visit. Our Ordnung bids us to be hospitable."

The offer was remarkably kind. So why did her fingers curl into a tight ball? Something cautioned her from bringing up Eileen's story, even though she itched to ask.

Annie rushed to the door, propping it open with her foot as Benjamin carried in a section of beadboard. He mostly averted his gaze as he brought it to the counter and carefully set it against the nearest wall. In the meantime, he cast a side glance at Annie. Her blond hair had slipped free of her braid, framing her face.

"Do you have something to say, Son?"

When Benjamin finally raised his gaze, with eyes just as blue as his father's and certainly far more stormy, he offered only a simple statement. "I am sorry for the misunderstanding."

Debbie would hardly call his rudeness a misunderstanding, but Daniel seemed satisfied as he placed a hand on his son's shoulder. "Gut, gut. You bring in the Blackthorn trim while I speak with Mrs. Albright about further business."

Benjamin left, but not before Debbie caught sight of his square jaw flexing. Interesting reaction. He didn't appear sorry. Had his father forced the apology?

"It's Miss Albright," Debbie corrected absently as she watched Benjamin leave the café with Annie trailing at arm's length.

Daniel's bushy eyebrows rose a fraction, and he leaned forward, his fingers resting against the curved glass. "I understand you received a letter from my *oncle*, Samuel. Would it be possible to view it?"

Ah. Now his generosity didn't seem so generous. She pushed away from the counter to give herself more space. "We don't have the letter anymore."

"Where is it?" Daniel's voice rose slightly, chasing away any previous attempt at friendliness. "I am a Lapp. I should be allowed to at least read it."

"I'm sorry, but as I previously shared with Hannah, Samuel addressed the letter to someone else."

He waved away her concern, as if it were nothing more than a bothersome gnat. "Yes, I know. Eileen Palmer."

"You're right. Eileen will have to give permission, or her daughter, Kim Smith. You could ask them. I know they would like to know what happened to your uncle Samuel."

Daniel's manner turned icy at Debbie's refusal. He sniffed. "Samuel Lapp abandoned his faith and left to fight in a war. He rejected our ways at the first pull of temptation."

Eileen, a temptation? Debbie didn't care to hear her friend described in such a callous manner. "You never heard from him again?"

Daniel shook his head, his mouth pursed as if he had tasted something bitter, and then he released a pained sigh. "Can you at least tell me if Samuel mentioned his family?"

She was tiptoeing across a delicate line, gathering information for her friend and, hopefully, not revealing too much in return. "The letter was solely for Eileen. A personal letter saying goodbye, if that helps."

Relief softened Daniel's mouth. He seemed satisfied with the answer. "Fair enough. I will not take up any more of your time. *Danki.*"

After he left, Annie motioned to the neatly stacked strips of unpainted trim and beadboard. "Should I put these in the storage room?"

Debbie nodded, distracted by Daniel's odd visit. She caught a glimpse of him and his son through the café windows. The buggy jolted forward, moving out of sight. "Check with Kim. Hopefully it's unlocked. I know we don't have room to store anything in the kitchen."

Annie picked up the smaller pieces. "I'll ask right now, if that's okay."

A middle-aged man at a nearby table raised his coffee cup, signaling he wanted more. Debbie picked up the coffeepot and weaved through the tables to refill his cup. As she poured the steaming coffee, a thought troubled her.

Why did Daniel appear relieved that the letter contained no mention of the Lapp family?

As Debbie and Janet locked up the café for the day, Kim waved from across the parking lot and started walking toward them. Judging by the familiar cars in the lot, most of the visitors had left, leaving only the museum staff.

"Did I hear correctly from Annie that you had an unusual visitor in the café?" Kim asked when she reached them. "I had to fend off her questions about Mom getting jilted. Your Annie insisted on seeing the letter again. She's quite the amateur historian, digging into the past. And then we got to talking about the history of the station. Perhaps I have her to thank, delaying me from running into Daniel Lapp."

Janet checked her watch. "Don't ask me about visitors. I was in the kitchen baking extra whoopie pies." She rolled her neck, no doubt working out the hours spent on the treats.

Debbie found her car keys, her dismay at the manipulative visit hard to shake. "I saw Daniel Lapp. He insisted he had a right to read the letter. I told him he would have to ask you or your mom."

Kim propped her fists on her hips. "Thank goodness he didn't ask me. If he had, I might have given him a piece of my mind."

"It does make me wonder why he's so distressed, especially after nearly eighty years," Debbie said. "Do you mind if I chat with your mom tonight? At least you'll both have a heads-up if he attempts a surprise visit."

"I'll come with you," Kim said. "I eat supper with Mom at least once a week."

"You ladies have a lovely night. I've got a date with Ian. I can't let him down, especially since it's so hard for him to get free time." Janet waved as she turned to her car.

As Debbie climbed behind the steering wheel, she saw a faded yellow Corvette with black racing stripes pull into the parking lot. Silas held open the main museum entrance for Annie. Judging from his scowling expression and raised voice, he appeared to be chiding her, but Debbie couldn't hear what he said.

Come to think of it, why was Annie the last one out of the building? Had she forgotten something? Her slim cross-body purse bounced against her hip as she darted out of the train station and jogged to the car, slipping inside before slamming the door shut. A dark-haired teenager sat in the driver's seat. Her brother? He turned on some music, and the car and everything around it vibrated with the bass notes. Then he peeled away, leaving streaks on the pavement, while a low-hanging tailpipe rattled and puffed out smoke.

Debbie grimaced at the noise as she drove out of the parking lot. Another thought made her tighten her grip on the steering wheel. Annie hadn't given an exact date for finishing her work at Whistle Stop. Surely she would need a few weeks to prepare to go back to college. As much as Debbie hated to lose the help, she resolved to have a conversation with the young woman as soon as possible. She needed to know if she had to find temporary help before September, when Paulette would return. But she could only focus on one person at a time, and right now it was Eileen's turn.

In the assisted living section of the retirement center, Debbie caught up with Kim and Eileen sitting at a round table, waiting for supper to be served to the residents. Debbie dragged a padded chair over and sat beside Eileen, greeting her with a smile and a hug. The brightly colored place mats and the floral centerpiece brought a touch of home, and several seniors waited around similar tables.

Debbie turned to Eileen. "Daniel Lapp came to the café today. He said he never heard from his uncle Samuel. He'd like to see the letter."

Kim put her hand on her mother's arm. "You don't have to let him see it."

Eileen lifted one thin shoulder. "Why not share it with him? I've lived a full and wonderful life. I'm grateful to get a letter from Samuel, but I'm sure I'm not the only one with questions about what happened to him."

Debbie leaned out of the way as one of the nursing home aides set a plate with grilled chicken, wild rice, and roasted asparagus in front of her. "Daniel was very curious to find out if Samuel mentioned the Lapp family in your letter."

Eileen sighed as she readjusted a linen napkin on her lap. "Well, isn't that something? I remember the Lapp family expressing no interest in finding their lost son. I tried to locate Samuel, but there were plenty of missing men following the war. The first five months after he enlisted, he answered my letters. But then his letters became sporadic, and I would go months without hearing anything. The Lapps shunned him before he left. And then, Elijah, his father, refused to reply to any of Samuel's letters. Samuel wrote that the only way he learned of home was through me. I tried to send something every month, just to keep him in the loop."

Debbie couldn't imagine blocking someone so completely from a family or a community. The consequences of such a devastating decision would reverberate through generations.

"Eat up." Eileen gestured with her fork to Debbie's untouched plate. "Dessert won't be as good as your whoopie pies, but it's bread pudding tonight. With caramel sauce and raisins."

Debbie sampled the grilled chicken. It was very good—a far better choice than the stale loaf of bread in her cupboard and a half-empty jar of peanut butter with oil pooling at the top. "I tried to find Richard Brown online as well, with no success. There are far too many Richard Browns who come up in an internet search."

"What did he look like?" Eileen asked as she delicately cut her asparagus into bite-sized pieces.

"Sandy-blond hair with a tinge of gray just above his ears. Well dressed, right down to his expensive Italian loafers. He drove a Jaguar, something we don't see too often in Dennison."

"I remember he had green eyes," Kim added as she cut her chicken into small pieces. "Startlingly green."

"Samuel had the bluest eyes I've ever seen," Eileen said as she set her fork next to her plate. "Light blond hair—almost white by the time summer ended. He loved to read. No one could get him enough books, not even the town library. He had to hide them in his room or in the barn loft since his father thought they were a sinful vanity and worldly."

"Was there speculation in the Amish community about what happened to him when he didn't return?" Debbie asked.

"There was. Some thought he had gone into hiding overseas. A few suggested he might be a deserter and would never dare show his face again in the Dennison and Sugarcreek communities. The Samuel I remember wasn't a coward, but then again, after this last letter, I'm not sure I knew him at all."

# CHAPTER TWELVE

My dear Samuel,

I hope you are well. My prayers are often with you. Life in Dennison goes on as always, but I miss you terribly. I've sent several letters, but I'm never quite certain you've received any of them. Since you left for the Pacific, I've tried to imagine your location to no success. I realize you can't send details.

Remember Margot, who oversees the canteen at the station? Her fiancé sends letters with blacked-out sections, hiding his location and plans. The last we heard, he was in a military hospital, possibly in London. She fears a gorgeous nurse will steal him with meals of bangers and mash. I assured her that the rations of sugar, meat, and tea we have in Dennison are likely just as severe in London.

Sometimes I fear you are trapped in a prisoner of war camp, or worse, and my letter will find its way to a forgotten pile, only to be discarded. Yet when my hope falls low, I remind myself of a favorite verse from Isaiah as I walk to work each morning.

"But they that wait upon the Lord shall renew their strength; they shall mount up with wings as eagles; they shall run, and not be weary; and they shall walk, and not faint."

Samuel, I am praying for you. Somehow, I feel in my heart that you are so very weary and alone. To be honest, I need the promise of strength too. The train station has become a second home to me, and I am grateful for the opportunity to serve the soldiers who pass through our doors. Yet there are days when it's all I can do to put one foot in front of the other. In the morning, the trains rattle in, bringing endless numbers of men. Bringing and taking every hour. Always taking, for most of the men and women I will never see again. So many of my classmates have left Dennison for the war effort. It feels as if we are constantly saying goodbye to someone. In those moments, I remember the wonderful times you and I shared, and it brings me hope.

In happier news, I found a stray kitten hiding beneath the platform next to the tracks. Buddy, our resident station dog, discovered the poor, shivering creature. I scooped up the tiny thing and snuggled him close. He is pure black—right down to his whiskers, nose, and paws. The roof of his mouth even has a patch of black. I named him Homer.

What an incredible journey this little one has endured. To think he's safe and warm—it gives me hope for you. He sits under my desk, sipping from a saucer of milk while the radio plays our song, "We'll Meet Again." Such throaty purrs. He has found his home. Margot keeps hinting about her need for a mouse hunter, but I'm not ready to part with him. I'm quite certain you would like Homer.

Write soon.

All my love,

Eileen

*Dennison, Ohio*
*May 1945*

*Why on earth had she decided to visit Samuel's home?*
*Eileen shivered despite the summer warmth as she*

turned the key in the ignition, killing the low clatter of the engine. A large, whitewashed house with a modest porch spread out before her, its many windows framed with shutters. As she shut the car door, her heels sank into the soft gravel driveway. The scent of grass filled the air with an irresistible aroma. Dragonflies danced on the breeze, zooming between wildflowers. A picture of tranquility. Yet her pulse raced all the same.

She was an Englischer, and she was about to intrude on a family who had never approved of her.

Once Samuel had taken her on a buggy ride, leading her past the Uhrichsville home and lumberyard. He had never offered to take her inside the spacious farmhouse. How ironic that, in his absence, she would formally visit the Lapp farm for the first time.

She noted the details, mentally composing a letter she might send later in the week. He would be pleased to hear that the house hadn't changed a bit. She climbed the steps and knocked on the door. Footsteps came toward her, and the door swung open, revealing Jacob's scowling face. He must have seen her approach.

He reached both arms to grip the doorframe, blocking her from entering. "Why are you here?"

Her mouth dried at his intimidating posture. Tall, with powerful shoulders and arms and that curling blond hair, which had proven to be her initial downfall.

*Unlike Samuel's warm blue gaze, Jacob glared at her with enough ice to freeze a pond in the springtime. Without a picture of Samuel to remember him by, she kept his memory close, but his image was blurry after two long years. Now, with Jacob in front of her, it felt as though Samuel had never left.*

*"I'm sorry to bother you, but I couldn't wait any longer. I've not heard from Samuel in a long time. Have you learned anything about him? I know he was deployed to the Pacific. I can't get any military department-ments or hospitals to answer my questions."*

*Jacob let go of the doorframe and shifted his stance. "You should know better than to come here. No one speaks his name within these walls. Go home."*

*Her fingers clenched into fists. "Have you heard nothing?"*

*He muttered something under his breath and ducked inside the house. He returned a moment later with grease-splattered papers which he thrust into her hands.*

*"What is this?"*

*"The top one is the* Budget. *It is our community's newspaper. Beneath it, you will find other local papers he submitted opinion letters to. Englischer papers. Your fool ideas and books made him believe he should fight and abandon everything and everyone he loved."*

She glanced at the papers in her hand, afraid of what she might read. "He wrote in these?"

Jacob narrowed his eyes. "You will find the last message we ever read from him at the top of the pile. He wrote about the need to seek freedom. From what, I wonder?"

Grief roiled in her, mingled with frustration over Jacob's unwillingness to understand his brother's point of view. "It's just that Samuel wanted so much more than an eighth-grade education. He longed to go to high school, and later, to college. It wasn't my dream. I've stayed in Dennison all my life, working different jobs in town until I was promoted to stationmaster. College and degrees and books aren't in my blood. How do you know he wouldn't have left on his own?"

"I know if he had not met you, he would not have had those fool ideas planted in his thick head." Jacob's expression was harsh and unyielding. "What is wrong with an eighth-grade education? It was gut enough for my daed, and it is gut enough for me. We did not need books to run a successful lumberyard."

When she didn't answer, he thumbed his suspenders, pulling them from his chest as he rocked on his heels. "I have got enough money saved to build a fine house of my own and provide for a wife. That is more than I can say for Samuel or any of those broken soldiers who limp home. Do not deny that you changed him with those books."

Building a fine house certainly didn't sound like plain talk, but she dared not contradict Jacob during such a tense moment. And the books had played a role, whether she wanted to admit it or not.

Eileen steeled herself against his obvious disdain. "All I'm asking is to know if Samuel is safe and alive. I'm not here to critique your way of life. We all lost him. Please, Jacob, I must know what happened to him."

His hands fell to his sides, and the rocking stopped. For a moment, a deep sorrow softened the granite planes of his face, and his gaze flickered away from hers. "Samuel is gone, and there is nothing we can do about it. Best carry on with your life and forget him. That is what I am going to do."

She could not so easily banish Samuel's memory from her thoughts. "I never meant for him to leave. I wanted him to stay in Dennison."

"Did you?" Jacob jabbed a finger in her direction. "If he had not gone to fight, the government would have forced him to the work camps reserved for conscientious objectors. I just returned home from Camp Elkton all the way from Oregon. My maam and daed had to run the mill without my help or Samuel's. You

*Englischers think only of yourselves, forcing the rest of us to do your selfish bidding."*

*She pressed her hand against her chest at the idea of young men shuffled off to camps against their will. Did he really speak the truth? "I didn't know. I-I'm so sorry." No wonder his expression remained so hateful, especially if he had to live so far from his family and community.*

*"So you keep saying. Good day, Eileen. At least spare my maam your presence. She hurts more than the rest of us."*

*"I am so sorry," Eileen whispered again as she backed away. Jacob slammed the door, and Eileen heard the sound of a deadbolt sliding into place. Rain drizzled, pattering against the roof of the porch. Numbly, she stared at the collection of papers.*

*The top one was dated November 10, 1943. News of weddings, babies, a barn raising, and other pleasant topics filled the first portion of the front page. Then she recognized Samuel's name. He wrote of several topics, including Gelassenheit—seeking God's will and submitting to it in the fullest sense, even to the point of great personal sacrifice. There was no mention of enlisting, yet the meaning was clear. He viewed fighting overseas as his sacrifice. Hot tears suddenly welled in her eyes, blurring the small print.*

Despite her sorrow, a cold thrill shot through her as Jacob's conversation replayed in her mind. Samuel had told her in his last letter—six months ago—that he had sent letters to the family, each missive ignored. But Jacob said this article from November 1943 was their last message from him—over eighteen months ago. Could she trust anything Jacob said? She couldn't believe Samuel would lie to her. As she left the porch, she saw a form move away from the window, drawing the curtain to shut out the light.

# CHAPTER THIRTEEN

**B**uona Vita on Sunday meant a restaurant full of regulars gathering for lunch after a rousing sermon from Pastor Nick Winston. Debbie searched the crowd, feeling slightly self-conscious. When Janet and Ian had invited her over for lunch, she had to explain she was meeting with Greg. Of course, that news made Ian smirk. Janet had merely given her a hug and promised a barbecue next week.

Debbie was about to head to the back section of the restaurant when the owner, Ricky Carosi, burst through the swinging doors dividing the kitchen from the dining area. His standard uniform, a black shirt and pants, made him as striking as ever, and he waved to her, drawing even more attention to himself. "Debbie! How are you? How's business at the café? My wife had coffee there the other day. I heard all about the giant cinnamon buns and the latest flavors of whoopie pies." He gestured with his hands to suggest the size of buns more in line with a bread loaf.

Debbie chuckled at his exaggeration. "Really? And we always hear from customers about your fabulous gelato and cannoli."

He spread his arms, eyes twinkling. "What can I say? Dennison has some of the most wonderful restaurants in Ohio." Ricky rubbed his hands together, his gold cuff links shining in the afternoon light. However, a pensive look crossed his face. "I hear that we have something in common with the depot. Did Ian tell you we had a break-in the other day? Thankfully, I was in the kitchen, and I must have scared the intruder off my property."

"That's terrible. We had antiques stolen last week."

Ricky ran a hand through his thick black hair. "Kids these days. Anyway, I won't keep you. You've got a gentleman waiting at a table. I hope you don't mind, but I seated you in the alcove. It's more private than my other booths." He raised his eyebrows as he directed her to a small table tucked away in the corner, hidden by an enormous fake fern.

"Oh, that's okay, Greg and I are just friends." The explanation gushed out of her, but Ricky had already turned to greet yet another customer, an elderly lady surrounded by her four clamoring grandchildren. Begging for gelato, no doubt.

*Smooth move, Debbie.* She didn't owe anyone an explanation about her relationship with Greg. But this thought was pushed to the back of her mind as the information Ricky shared made the hair on the back of her neck prickle. Dennison was a safe community, perfect for young families and retired individuals. Who would break into a beloved restaurant like Buona Vita?

She shook off the feeling and made her way over to Greg, who gazed out the window. She'd seen him in church earlier, and he hadn't changed from his Sunday clothes either. He stood up when he saw her, his smile just as welcoming as Ricky's. She immediately relaxed.

"Glad you could make it," he said as he pulled out a chair for her.

"I'm grateful you could meet with me. My mind has been racing over different scenarios, and I'd love some insight. By the way, where are your boys?"

He sat back down. "Pastor Nick is having the youth group over for a cookout today. One last hurrah before school starts. I'm about worn out trying to keep up with their energy."

She didn't believe it for a moment. Greg's work schedule put most people to shame.

When Ricky came to the table, they both ordered the special, eggplant parmigiana. After Ricky left, Debbie leaned forward, keeping her voice soft as she explained Eileen's story and the visit to Lapp Lumber.

"Do you know anything about Samuel Lapp?" she asked. "Or maybe someone who might know how to find him? I've tried searching for Richard Brown, but I haven't found anything. It's like trying to find a needle in a haystack."

Greg tapped his fingers against his water glass. "Have you spoken with Harry? Of course, you could check the historical archives at the library and see if there's anything there that would help."

Harry Franklin had worked as a porter at the depot during the war. He had proven to be immensely helpful with his recollection of past details about the station and the people who worked there.

"I'm open to it. But I don't have a photo or much of anything to work with since Samuel was Amish. The envelope didn't have a return address. And it was never sent. It appears as if he wrote the letter and kept it with him for years. Perhaps a fellow soldier kept it in case Samuel was killed in action. There wasn't even a postage stamp."

"How did Richard Brown get the letter?" Greg asked. "My grandmother kept the letters, postcards, and notes from my grandfather safe in the family Bible. It's quite the historical treasure, dating back to the Civil War, with lists of all the family descendants. It's got Sunday school lessons, clippings of old newspapers, dried flowers even, between the pages."

Greg's grandfather had gone missing and never came back from the war, and his mention of the keepsakes in his grandmother's Bible pricked Debbie's memory. Hadn't Kim said that Richard was keenly interested in Eileen's mementos on display at the station? And Kim had mentioned helping her mother reorganize scrapbooks.

Debbie inhaled sharply. Could Richard have some sort of family connection to Samuel Lapp, or Eileen? Had Eileen revealed everything, or would additional secrets be uncovered?

When Ricky brought out a plate of cannoli, the sweet cream oozing from the golden shells, Greg groaned. "I don't know how I could possibly eat another bite."

Ricky bowed with a flourish. "It's on the house, and many more in the future, I hope. Thanks to you, I now have a repaired window."

Debbie raised a brow. "Was the window broken by the intruder?"

Greg nodded as he grabbed the spoon resting on his napkin to sample the cannoli. "Yep. Ian and the police department know about it. They're planning to increase their patrols around businesses over the next few weeks."

"Kids, I tell you," Ricky said, shaking a finger as if he was itching to scold teenagers.

Debbie folded her napkin. She couldn't eat another bite, not when she felt so tense. She forced herself to sip her ice water and wait for Greg to finish the dessert.

"I wonder who would be bold enough to do something so outlandish to Ricky," she murmured over her glass.

Greg set his spoon on the plate. "I don't know. My boys some-times hear of kids doing stupid stuff, like having underage drinking parties in abandoned buildings. Or maybe a foolish prank at Halloween. I think one kid in tenth grade egged the high school principal's car a few weeks ago—a kid named Nicholas Butler, if I remember correctly. All in good fun, he insisted, but the car's finish was ruined. So far Jaxon hasn't heard anything about the recent theft and vandalizing. But this doesn't sound like the shenanigans of rowdy kids to me."

"I'll take a peek at Ricky's back door and let Kim know what I see. Maybe there'll be some similarities." Debbie's mind whirled as she considered what Greg had shared. Nicholas Butler? As in Annie's brother? Egging a car wasn't just harmless mischief.

"I'll come with you."

Ricky led her and Greg through the swinging doors of the kitchen. The Carosi family had owned the business for decades—a favorite eatery of Dennison's residents and tourists alike. Ricky led them outside, behind the restaurant, and gestured at the exterior of the building.

"I rarely lock the back door when I'm working, but now I'll have no choice."

"Floodlights with an automatic timer might help," Greg offered as he inspected the door and window. "Or motion sensor lights."

"What did Ian say about all this? Does he have any leads yet?" Debbie asked as she touched the freshly painted wood siding. The new window sparkled. Could this break-in be linked to the train station robbery? She hated the idea of someone out there damaging property and hurting her friends.

Ricky frowned. "No leads. Ian believes we have a few teenagers with too much time on their hands. Yesterday, I purchased security cameras from an online store, but I won't get them for another two weeks. An irritating delay, if you ask me."

"Kim ordered security cameras as well," Debbie said. "I wonder if someone wanted to steal cash." How sad that her friends had to take such precautions. The presumption of safety in a small town had drawn her back here after living in a bustling city, where she was always looking over her shoulder.

"I don't leave colossal sums of cash overnight in the restaurant," Ricky said. "My wife makes a bank deposit at the end of every workday."

A ringtone caught everyone's attention. Greg pulled out his phone and answered it. He sighed when he ended the call. "Julian twisted his ankle on Pastor Nick's trampoline." He glanced at Debbie with a hopeful expression. "I could go with you another time to visit Harry. Coffee and dessert included?"

"I'd love that," she agreed after a pause. Life was plenty busy, but a little coffee and dessert didn't hurt anyone. Especially with a friend like Greg Connor.

## CHAPTER FOURTEEN

*D*ebbie's phone dinged late Sunday night. She picked it up, pleased to see a text from Kim.

DEBBIE, YOUR ADVICE WAS ON TARGET. MOM HAS A KEEPSAKE PRESSED IN AN OLD SCRAPBOOK. BLESS HER HEART. SHE HAD FORGOTTEN ALL ABOUT IT. I'M GOING TO SEND YOU A PHOTO IN JUST A SECOND. I THINK YOU'LL FIND IT USEFUL.

Debbie grinned at the smiley face emoji following the text. She had left a message for Kim to check any stored boxes or books for mementos of Samuel. However, all credit went to Greg for the mini breakthrough.

I'M SO GLAD YOU FOUND SOMETHING, she typed back, waiting for the speech bubble to pop up and show Kim's response.

Debbie had feared she might face a dead end and be forced to admit defeat. She couldn't deny that the search for Eileen's lost beau had morphed into something personal, reminding her of Reed and the season of sorrow his loss had brought.

The phone dinged again, and a picture came through. Debbie zoomed in on the detail. The photo revealed a newspaper article, yellowed with age.

Kim's response soon appeared below the photo.

SAMUEL WROTE A FEW DEVOTIONAL PIECES AND LETTERS TO THE EDITORS FOR THE AMISH NEWSPAPER AND SOME ENGLISH

PAPERS. HIS WRITING IS VERY GOOD. MOM CRIED WHEN I READ HIS SECTIONS OUT LOUD. SHE SAYS SHE HID THE PAPERS BECAUSE IT HURT SO MUCH. I GUESS SHE FORGOT ABOUT THEM.

Debbie tucked her feet under her as she leaned against the velvet couch cushions. She read an open letter to the *Budget* editor, mulling over the words. One particular line struck her, the sentiment resonating deep within her soul.

*Do we not seek God's will in every area of our lives? Do we not release our gifts to Him to serve as He sees fit? Surely it is foolishness to be the fearful man who buries a talent in the field when his fellow workers boldly invest and use their talents for God's glory. Who receives the greater reward?*

She had wrestled with a similar idea when deliberating whether to leave the city and risk opening the café. Did she trust God enough to release her gifts to be used as He saw fit? Her former coworkers had raised eyebrows when she had shared her dream of a lovely place to visit with old friends while enjoying baked goods and coffee. To be able to contribute to the community and find belonging had brought her home after so many years. Yet the risk of the unknown had sometimes seemed too great a weight to bear.

If Samuel felt the same way she did, what gifts did he mean?

On Monday afternoon Debbie and Janet headed to Harry's house. Debbie had called him in the morning, asking for a quick chat. Harry had readily agreed, teasing that she needed to bring treats.

She glanced at the neat yard and small cottage as Janet parked the car. A rose garden, complete with a charming white arbor overrun with trailing vines, welcomed visitors. Harry waited on the front porch in a rocking chair, a cane resting beside him. Crosby, his faithful companion, perked up and offered a friendly bark, tail wagging. Crosby was descended from the famed World War I dog, Bing, who had survived his battle wounds and had returned to Dennison to live out the rest of his days.

"I can't imagine a more lovely way to spend an afternoon," Janet said as she sniffed the fragrant blossoms nearest to her. Pink and yellow roses bloomed in profusion, scattering petals across the sidewalk.

Debbie waved at Harry and joined him on the porch while Janet sat on another rocking chair opposite him. Trees rustled overhead, and a small birdbath drew birds to the edge to drink.

"Good afternoon, ladies," Harry said. He wore a pair of beige slacks, brown shoes, and a green plaid shirt with short sleeves.

"You look very dapper, Harry," Debbie said. "By the way, we missed seeing you and Crosby at the station last week. Are you doing okay?"

He sighed heavily. "I'm getting over a nasty cold, and my granddaughter insisted I stay away from the visitors at the station. I told her she worries too much. How else am I going to get cinnamon buns, if not from you?"

Debbie grinned as she handed over a small paper bag filled with baked goods. "Cookies for information?"

He laughed as he opened the bag and examined the contents. "Hmm. Oatmeal raisin. My, you really know how to bribe a man. I accept. You mentioned Samuel Lapp over the phone."

"We'll drop off lunch anytime," Janet promised. "Do you remember Samuel from your days serving the train station?"

"I sure do. That boy was plumb crazy for Eileen Turner. He'd swing by the station in that buggy of his and find some excuse or another to see her. They'd meet at the park, or at the Revco drugstore during his rumspringa. Headstrong boy, if I ever saw one. One day, when I was taking a break outside with a newspaper in hand, he asked if he could take a quick peek at it. I gave it to him, listening as he oohed and aahed over the articles. Sometimes he'd ask my opinion on current events. His papa didn't like a hankering for that kind of reading. Said why bring the wicked world into their home? But after I shared that first one, Samuel would find me at the station every week and ask if he could have the paper once I finished reading it."

"What do you mean by headstrong?" Janet asked.

Harry folded his hands over his cane. "He didn't take no for an answer. Not when he really wanted something, like my newspaper. You realize that by courting Eileen, he defied his papa, old Elijah Lapp."

"Did you know he wrote opinion and devotional pieces for the *Budget* and for some English papers as well?" Debbie asked.

"No. But I'm not surprised. He wouldn't stop pestering me with questions about the paper. Quiet, serious, but curious about the world outside Sugarcreek." Harry patted his cane. "He never complained about his Amish family, but I often wondered if he was secretly restless. Just before he enlisted, I thought he watched the trains more than Eileen. You have to look out for those deep thinkers. They don't let you know what's going on beneath the surface. It's a shame he never returned home. Eileen, God bless her, managed the station to the best of her ability. But we all knew she grieved sorely."

A picture of Eileen in her younger days filled Debbie's mind. From all accounts, the former stationmaster had been hardworking, kindhearted, and generous. Yet the photo on display at the station revealed a certain sadness in her eyes, and a tentative smile full of uncertainty. How unfortunate to be searching for someone's return and never hearing a word. To be always waiting and waiting.

The image of a brown-haired man wearing army fatigues flashed through Debbie's mind. She didn't want to think about Afghanistan right now, yet despite her best efforts, a shudder rippled through her. After promising to bring Harry more oatmeal raisin cookies and a cinnamon roll or two, Debbie and Janet left.

"Were you all right back there?" Janet asked when they reached the car.

"I'm fine. Truly. I'm thinking about Eileen handling such tough news at her age. She's the one we need to be checking with."

"Mm-hmm." Janet squinted, as if she were looking right through Debbie.

Debbie walked to the other side of the car and opened the door, eager to take the focus off herself. She hoped Janet wouldn't bring up Reed along with the concept of moving forward in life. Hadn't she moved forward enough?

Thankfully, Janet didn't breathe a word about Reed as she reached the driver's side.

"Do you believe Daniel never learned what happened to Samuel? I find it hard to swallow that Jacob and Elijah heard nothing from him. Didn't Samuel's letter say he tried to contact his family?

Wouldn't the War Department have sent word if he'd been killed or missing in action?" The wind played with Janet's blond bob.

"Someone wants to hide the truth. We just don't know who yet," Debbie said.

Might Samuel's parents have received letters and hidden them from their family? Hannah had proved herself helpful when her brother wasn't around to censor her conversation. Perhaps a second visit to Lapp Lumber was in order.

# CHAPTER FIFTEEN

*L*ate Tuesday afternoon Debbie parked her car in front of the Uhrichsville branch of the Claymont library, where she had agreed to meet Janet after closing the café. Annie had waved Debbie and Janet out of the café, promising to take care of everything.

Janet waited on the sidewalk next to the library. Her black T-shirt said YOU HAD ME AT BAKING and bore evidence of sugar icing thanks to another busy day at the café.

Debbie hid a smile at her friend's quirky fashion. Her own outfit bore plenty of grease stains from making Reuben sandwiches and a special order of grilled cheese for a few picky eaters in one young family. "Maybe we should have changed before coming here."

Janet glanced down at her cuffed jeans and leopard-print sneakers. "You know, I thought of ordering you the same shirt. We could match at the café."

Debbie smirked. "I appreciate your attempts at changing my fashion." She wasn't sure she could pull off Janet's flair for the whimsical.

"One of these days, I'll get you to relax."

"Ha!" Debbie said as she walked through the library doors. The air-conditioning felt good after the sweltering heat outside. The historic building was charming, with reading nooks and cozy chairs along with several narrow wooden tables. The scent of books, sweet and musty, mingled with lemony cleaner, brought back a rush of memories from childhood when she'd sat at a similar table, devouring the latest escapades of Ramona Quimby.

A cough came from behind a bookshelf. Debbie turned to see the librarian, Julie Caldwell, point toward the archive room behind a row of tall shelves.

"You'll find plenty of quiet time to study," she said as she adjusted her purple glasses. A vibrant purple and red scarf hung around her neck, matching her oversized amethyst earrings and vibrant red hair. "But let me go clean up from the last person who was in there so you can find what you need."

"Is someone else digging into Dennison history?" Janet asked.

Julie nodded, her fiery curls bouncing. "Yes, it's quite the coincidence when you think about it. He had a similar fascination with World War II history and the train station."

Debbie's arms flared with goose bumps. "Did you know who he was?"

"I'm not allowed to say. He came to visit the library a few weeks ago. Didn't find what he was looking for, I guess. I received a call from him this morning, and he asked if he could come again this afternoon."

Janet's eyes widened. "You don't suppose it's Richard Brown, do you?"

Debbie glanced at Julie in time to see the startled look on her face. Julie smiled. "I wouldn't be a bit surprised."

Debbie held her breath as she zoomed in on the screen displaying a microfiche file. "Doesn't this monitor remind you of our computer class in high school? Remember floppy disks?"

Janet snorted as she found a chair to pull up beside Debbie. "I hated that class."

"Julie says the microfiche files can be stored as long as five hundred years if the temperatures stay stable. Pretty impressive," Debbie said. A stack to her left waited to be explored. Julie had agreed that, although she couldn't give out any personal information about the history-seeking patron, she could wait until they left to return the files he looked at to their proper place.

Janet leaned over her to read the fine print on the monitor. The soft swivel chair creaked beneath Debbie as she studied the enlarged headline. A small brass clock on the wall ticked steadily.

*On February 19, 1945, some 30,000 United States Marines landed on the western Pacific island of Iwo Jima, where they bravely countered ferocious resistance from Japanese forces. Despite the challenge, American soldiers seized control of the strategically important island after a month-long battle that ended on March 26. Their valiant effort was not without cost. Many men are reported missing, injured, or deceased.*

*Just four days into the fighting, brave US Marines captured Mount Suribachi, on Iwo Jima's south side, defiantly raising an American flag at the summit. Associated Press photographer Joe Rosenthal, who won a Pulitzer Prize for the famous photograph, captured the breathless moment of triumphant marines at the peak of the mountain.*

The article went on to paint a picture of that iconic moment that had Debbie almost in tears. She raised her eyes to the top of the page to see the author's byline and was surprised to see "the Unnamed Soldier" written there.

The door to the archive room creaked open, and Julie entered. "Are you all finding what you need?" she asked.

Debbie pointed to the computer screen. "Do you know anything about this journalist who goes by 'the Unnamed Soldier'? He's extraordinary."

"You're not the first to be interested in him today," Julie said with a pointed look. "The major newspapers are the ones that nicknamed the writer the Unnamed Soldier. At the time no one knew his true identity, and as far as I know, that's still true. I did some digging on my own and discovered that the Unnamed Soldier also wrote for the *New York Times* and the *Atlantic* and several other prestigious papers overseas."

"Goodness," Debbie said as she swiveled back to the microfiche. "That's fascinating."

"Isn't it? I'd really like to know who the man was. His identity alone would be newsworthy for any historical society or museum. He described the foul conditions in the field hospitals and helped increase awareness to improve health care for the soldiers. He also wrote lighter stories for the newspapers when the world felt like it was falling apart. One of the more famous articles described a group of soldiers singing hymns at Christmas and Easter, boosting public morale. He often depicted the children he encountered, especially the orphans, and encouraged the rest of the world to care about their fate. In fact, there were rumors that this man might have been nominated for the Pulitzer for journalism, but no one knew who to give the award to."

"A herald of hope during a dark time in history," Janet said, her voice holding a hint of awe.

Debbie cleared her throat, hoping what she was going to suggest would be acceptable. "Julie, I don't want you to do anything against your policies, but would it be possible for you to get in touch with the man who was researching here before us and ask him if he'd be willing to talk to us?"

Julie nodded. "I can call him. He didn't give me his email address. I can explain that you have an avid interest in World War II stories, and maybe the three of you could pool resources."

It wasn't an optimal option, but it was probably the most ethical. Debbie scribbled her phone number and email address on a slip of paper and handed it to Julie. "Let's keep Eileen out of the conversation as much as we can. I can't help but feel protective of her."

Janet rubbed her temples after Julie left the room. "Maybe there's another way we can contact Richard, whoever he is. We should have a backup plan in case Julie can't get ahold of him."

"I couldn't find him with an internet search. But he showed a huge interest at the museum with his questions for Kim. Could he have signed up for the museum's newsletter?"

Janet brightened. "That's possible. Let me call her and find out if he's in the system. Then maybe she would send him a carefully worded email and see if she can lure him out of hiding." She moved to the windows to make the call.

Debbie returned to the microfiche, and a curious thought struck her. She pulled out her phone and did a quick Google search. *Richard Brown journalist World War II.*

Surely it couldn't be that easy, could it?

It wasn't. She leaned back in the chair, ignoring the protesting creak. Could Samuel have survived the war? His letter hinted that he served in the Pacific. Did the Unnamed Soldier know Samuel? Could the Unnamed Solder *be* Samuel? She remembered her visit with Cheryl from Sugarcreek. So far, every lead had proven disappointing. Cheryl hadn't called her back with any news about the other Amish soldier that was shunned by his family. Could these men have encountered each other during the war?

She rubbed her chin, deep in thought.

Another story stole her attention.

*The men who raised the American flag on Iwo Jima were Navy Pharmacist's Mate John Bradley, Sgt. Michael Strank, Cpl. Rene Gagnon, Cpl. Harlon Block, Cpl. Ira Hayes, and PFC Franklin Sousley. The Pulitzer-prizewinning picture becomes even more poignant when we realize that three of these men, Block, Strank, and Sousley, were killed before the battle for Iwo Jima was over.*

She propped her chin as she read the rest of the article. Why was Richard Brown interested in Iwo Jima?

"Thank you, Kim! You are brilliant as always." Janet ended her phone call and slipped her phone into her back pocket. Her eyes shone with excitement. "The answer is yes. She says she'll come to the café tomorrow and we can get an email sent to him."

# CHAPTER SIXTEEN

*Dennison, Ohio*
*October 1945*

*"I'm looking for the nearest restaurant that serves a decent meal with homemade pie. Do you know how long it's been since I've had a proper slice of apple pie?"*

*A voice as rich as chocolate cream drew Eileen's attention from her train schedule. She raised her head and caught the glance of a tall man in uniform leaning against the ticket counter, his fingers tapping a restless beat against the polished wood. He lowered his voice, and Eileen could no longer hear the conversation between the ticket attendant and the stranger.*

*The attendant, a young girl named Nancy, blushed bright red from behind the framed counter. "N-no sir. Maybe the Revco drugstore?"*

*Eileen winced at the idea of a drugstore offering a hearty meal to a soldier in need. Milkshakes and sodas, yes. Candy, of course. Steaks and pie, hardly.*

*"Go to Buona Vita," she blurted, her voice ringing across the tiled floor. "You definitely want to go there. He serves the finest meals in town. If you hurry now, you'll catch him before closing. I've never known Alberto to turn down a hungry man in uniform."*

*While the other returning soldiers didn't exactly take to Italian meals—an unfortunate consequence of the war—Eileen did her best to support the new restaurant every chance she got. She especially liked Alberto Carosi and his quirky sense of humor. She wanted to do whatever she could to make the Carosi family feel at home in Dennison, Ohio.*

*The man slowly turned around, giving Eileen a view of his face. No wonder Nancy stuttered like a schoolgirl. Tanned, with a rakish manner. He offered a slow smile when he saw Eileen. She stiffened, noting his neatly pressed, olive-hued uniform and the military decorations declaring him to be a marine. The chevron plaque on his sleeve indicated an elevated rank, but she wasn't certain which one.*

*"Sicilian Italian?" the man asked, as if challenging her.*

*Bristling, she held her clipboard like a shield. "Alberto hails from Little Italy, New York. If you like Sicilian cooking, he's your man. He makes perfect cannoli, and he'll likely have apple pie or something good this late at night. But if you prefer, I can recommend other places."*

*He shook his head. "No, Buona Vita it is." He picked up the suitcase resting on the floor and sauntered over to her. Oh my. He wasn't as handsome as Samuel—not with that faint scar on the left temple, cutting into a thick eyebrow, but there was a certain undeniable spark to him, which made it difficult for her to look away. She admonished herself against appearing too friendly.*

*A twinkle appeared in his eyes. "You wouldn't happen to be free for dinner, would you?"*

*Eileen swallowed, her mouth suddenly dry. She ignored Nancy's quiet titter behind the ticket counter. Goodness. Eileen felt tongue-tied when he stopped in front of her. She had refused dates before with plenty of gentle but firm tact. In fact, the last proper date she'd had was at the Revco drugstore with Samuel, sharing vanilla milkshakes.*

*She brushed aside the memory. "I'm afraid not, Mr—"*

*"Palmer. Rafe Palmer." He reached out with his long arm, and before she could stop herself, she was*

shaking his hand. His grip was firm. Thankfully, he didn't hold her hand too long.

"Mr. Palmer, you have enough time to eat and be back before the last train leaves for the night."

He tilted his head, studying her. "Oh, I won't be leaving. I'm planning on staying in Dennison. There's plenty to commend this beautiful town, from what I've heard."

She opened her mouth and promptly shut it. Questions flooded her. Where would he stay? What would he do? Did he have family in town? But the answers were none of her business. So many men came through the train station. Although she tried to be kind to each person she encountered, most of the faces blurred together, with only one face remaining in her memory. Rafe Palmer would disappear from her life as so many others had.

Instead of engaging in further conversation, she nodded briskly, keeping her voice cool. "Welcome to Dennison, Mr. Palmer."

# CHAPTER SEVENTEEN

ebbie glanced at the clock on the wall of the café Wednesday morning. Annie was late, an unusual occurrence. She stepped outside. Kim's van and Janet's car were in the parking lot, but no sign of Annie.

When she dialed Annie's number, her call went straight to voice mail. As of yet, Annie hadn't given a date for quitting work and hadn't said anything more about Ohio State. Struggling to curb her frustration, Debbie filled the coffee maker with water and scooped the right amount of ground coffee before pressing the start button. The machine hissed and stuttered, the sound of percolating filling the silence.

Janet was in the kitchen, trying her hand at kuchen again. Naomi's recipe had worked fairly well, but Janet remained convinced something better existed in Amish country, and she wouldn't rest until she found the perfect recipe. Janet hadn't received anything in the mail from Hannah Lapp yet.

The radio in the kitchen switched on, playing Bing Crosby, and Janet hummed along.

When Debbie entered the kitchen, she suppressed a giggle at the sight of her friend swaying to the music while placing thin slices of apples in neat layers around a circle of dough. If anyone showcased pure joy while cooking, it was Janet.

"Baking is your gift, my friend," Debbie said.

"Just as number crunching is yours. Grab me the cinnamon, will you?" Janet carefully nudged more apples into place. "We'll try the apple today. Maybe peach or cherry kuchen tomorrow. If this fails, I'm baking more half-moon pies."

Amish half-moon pies, which were essentially handheld apple pies, might become Debbie's new favorite snack. She grabbed a glass jar filled with aromatic cinnamon. It had come all the way from Mexico, according to the label.

"That's Ceylon cinnamon. Not as harsh as the cassia cinnamon we think of as regular cinnamon. Cane sugar next, please." Janet loved to teach cooking whenever she had a chance. Debbie really enjoyed learning from her.

She found the sugar and passed it to Janet, who added it to the cinnamon before sprinkling the mixture over the thinly layered apples.

"Speaking of crunching numbers," Debbie said, "I'm nervous about the fall and winter months when we have fewer tourists. I'm wondering if we can supply desserts to some of the surrounding businesses, like the gas stations and grocery stores. Eileen mentioned how much the assisted-living residents love your baking. What if we contracted with Good Shepherd to offer regular treats?"

Between the mystery of Eileen's lost soldier and the latest accounting numbers, including profit margins and expenses, Debbie had spent a few sleepless nights stewing over how to best use her strengths. She had savings in the bank, but she would prefer not to dip into her precious and hard-earned reserve. The craftsman home, although charming, had brought a few recent hefty bills, despite her father and Greg working hard to help her cut costs.

She rubbed her dry eyes, the ache intensifying along with her worries.

*Lord, can You make a way through these pressing issues? I don't know what to do. I'm feeling more and more overwhelmed.*

Janet nodded as she sidestepped toward the stove, where a saucepan waited with a host of ingredients Debbie didn't even recognize. "I love the idea. You set up the deliveries, and I'll bake more. By the way, where is our helper?" She turned the dial to heat the pot and picked up a wooden spoon.

"Late, which isn't like her. Honestly, the more the month stretches on, the more distracted she seems."

"I'm sure she's just got her mind on packing and what she needs for college," Janet said. "Tiffany is just as distracted these days." She added a dash of something from a brown bottle. The warm scent of vanilla filled the kitchen, mingling with the sweet cinnamon.

"I'm sure you're right." Debbie set Janet's dirty measuring cups in the dishwasher before adding a detergent pod and pressing the start button.

"Who's right?" Annie appeared in the doorway, her cheeks bright red without the help of makeup. Her hair hung in loose, damp waves, as if she had just stepped out of the shower. Her wrinkled white T-shirt and baggy cargo pants were a far cry from her usual outfits. Her nylon backpack hung from one shoulder.

"There you are!" Debbie said. "We weren't sure what happened to you. Is everything all right?"

"Car trouble. It won't happen again, I promise." Annie hung up her bag and reached for an apron dangling from a hook, averting her face from Debbie and Janet.

"Speaking of cars, Kim noticed the tread marks from the tires when the Corvette peeled out of the parking lot. She wasn't pleased." Debbie didn't want to add to Annie's stress, but Kim had expressed concern, and it needed to be addressed sooner rather than later.

Annie wiped what looked like a tear away with the back of her hand. "Of course. It's my brother's car, and he gets enthusiastic behind the wheel. I'll tell him the next time I see him. He's a good kid, and he means well."

Debbie nodded. "Have you heard any word from Ohio State?"

Annie readjusted her apron ties to fit her narrow waist. "Uh, hopefully soon. I'm just waiting for some paperwork to arrive in the mail."

Hadn't she said the same thing over a week ago?

Debbie glanced at the calendar pinned to the wall. Annie didn't have much time before fall registration would begin. And if she was going to move into a dorm, that would have to happen soon. Something wasn't adding up. If Annie wasn't planning to go to Ohio State, why not just come clean and admit it?

"Mom says it's okay to give the letter to the Lapps." Kim handed the fragile envelope to Debbie later that morning. "Considering the family history, I'm not sure I'm the one who should do it. Do you mind taking it to Daniel? Hopefully, Benjamin won't be so boorish."

Debbie looked at the clock and wiped her hands on her apron before reaching for the envelope. "I don't mind. I'll take it to the Lapps tomorrow after work. How's your mom feeling about Samuel's letter?"

Annie scrubbed tables, cleaning the crumbs and smeared icing. She tilted her head at Debbie then resumed her work.

Debbie held the thin envelope in her hand, marveling at all the trouble it was causing decades after it was written. Maybe the letter would prove to be a peace offering. Besides, she wouldn't mind the opportunity to ask more questions. During her lunch break, she and Kim had drafted a quick email to Richard Brown. Kim had offered more information to Richard about her mom as a hook. Eager for answers, she had also included her phone number and Debbie's.

Kim folded her arms across her chest, her expression resolute. "Mom's sad, of course. She's been pretty tight-lipped over the story, but now and then she'll share a new tidbit. She says it's fine if she doesn't get the letter returned, and it's far too personal to put in the museum. I took a picture of it and also made a few copies, just in case I never see it again. Maybe it will bring a sense of closure to the Lapp family."

Debbie nodded, thinking of Samuel sharing sensitive information. Had he actually sent the letter, censors would have cut details useful to the enemy.

"It's interesting that Samuel kept the letter. Why not destroy it? Or better yet, why not send it and give Eileen relief, even if a year or two later?" His actions felt almost cruel, leaving Eileen dangling for an answer as to his fate.

Janet joined the conversation with a tea towel slung over her shoulder. "Tiffany told me about a terrible trend of 'ghosting' a boyfriend or girlfriend. It's so different from how Ian and I dated, but I was also wondering why Samuel kept the letter with him all these years. Why didn't he simply throw it in the trash can and get on with his life?"

Kim raised an eyebrow. "What on earth do you mean by 'ghosting'?"

Janet rolled her eyes. "It's when a boy or girl loses interest and never sends a text or calls to end the relationship. They just move on to the next one. I'm learning many interesting things about dating life from Tiffany. Thankfully, my girl has good discernment when it comes to that stuff."

"Growing up seeing a healthy relationship certainly helps with discernment," Kim agreed. "I still remember my father insisting on dating Mom well after they were married and with me in tow. He said he needed my mother to share adventures with. He would leave flowers and notes on the kitchen table or surprise her with concert tickets, just for the two of them. He was full of romantic gestures."

Debbie noticed Annie lingering over wiping a table, the rag clutched in her hand. Then she lifted the plastic ice cream bucket with soapy water and moved to a closer table. Was she eavesdropping? Maybe she had some boyfriend trouble as well.

Kim didn't appear to notice Annie's proximity. "I've been thinking a lot about Samuel. Did he die or go missing in the war? Or did he jilt my mom and disappear?"

Debbie slipped Samuel's letter into her apron pocket. "I'm very intrigued by Richard Brown's involvement. Why did he have

Samuel's letter? Why is he so interested in the Unnamed Soldier who wrote for the big papers?"

"Mom didn't answer her phone when I called to see if she knows anything," Kim said. "I'm sure she was napping or playing bingo in the common area. I want that information for the museum, if possible."

Janet swung the towel, her brows furrowed. "Whoever finds the unknown journalist's identity could receive nationwide recognition. From what Julie told us, his writing touched a lot of lives during the war and after."

Debbie raised her hands in mock surrender. "Too many missing men to locate. Too many secret identities. But I agree. Somehow, we'll dig into each lead. By the way, any word on the missing antiques?"

Kim inhaled sharply. "No. I've hunted everywhere for them."

Annie straightened from her work. "I'm sorry, but I couldn't help but overhear the conversation. My brother said he saw an Amish buggy a few nights ago driving out of Buona Vita. I'm sure it was nothing...but it terrified him. He nearly rear-ended the buggy because the reflector on the bumper was broken."

Debbie frowned. "Did your brother get a good look at the driver?"

Annie shook her head. "No. He thought it was a younger man driving alone. Nicholas said it was strange anyone was there, since Buona Vita was definitely closed."

"Tell your brother thank you for being more careful when he's driving. My parking lot thanks him as well." Kim smiled.

Annie, who seemed at ease with Kim's gentle humor, glanced at Debbie. "I'm sure it could be anyone. There are a lot of Amish families around here. And it might be nothing suspicious. Maybe just a wrong turn late at night."

Janet turned to go back to her baking. "You're right, Annie. It could be anyone."

But Debbie wasn't so sure. Why would a young man be driving a buggy late at night? And more importantly, could it have been Benjamin Lapp?

# CHAPTER EIGHTEEN

Someone tapped Debbie's shoulder shortly after the lunch rush, drawing her away from washing the sticky counter. The interruption was a welcome distraction. For the rest of the morning, Debbie had mulled over Annie's concern about a buggy out late at night and Kim's musings on the Unnamed Soldier.

"Ian told me to buy the curio cabinet—the one at Lapp Lumber," Janet said as she removed her hairnet and apron after a busy day of baking and making sandwiches. A faint imprint ringed her forehead like a halo. She brushed away a few stray crumbs from a lime-green T-shirt that read I LIKE TO PARTY, AND BY PARTY, I MEAN BAKE COOKIES. "It's perfect for our entrance here. I just hope we get those antique kitchen gadgets back so we can put them in it."

Debbie wrapped her arm around her friend, touched by Ian's generosity. "Please thank Ian for me. I wanted it the moment I saw it, but I'm currently strapped for cash."

Janet returned the hug. "We're in this business together. I love the cabinet as much as you do. Besides, we really need to visit Lapp Lumber again, since we promised Kim that we would show them the letter. I never got a kuchen recipe from Hannah, and I really want to try it. Naomi and Cheryl offered good recipes, but I can't shake the feeling that I'm missing out on something wonderful. Call it intuition. Why don't we see if the Lapp men are in a better mood tomorrow afternoon? I think we can leave right after closing time."

Debbie nodded. "I've been itching to revisit Lapp Lumber, and this provides the perfect excuse."

"Excellent." Janet refilled her travel mug with fresh coffee from the coffeepot. She flipped the switch to the off position. "I've been thinking about Kim's questions about Samuel's writing in the Amish paper and Richard Brown's fascination with the Unnamed Soldier who wrote for the major papers. Do you think Samuel and the Unnamed Soldier somehow knew each other? Did they fight together? Correspond with each other?"

Debbie had pondered the same questions. She also wondered if Samuel could be the Unnamed Soldier. Before she could answer, her attention was momentarily diverted.

In the dining section, Annie nearly tripped as she balanced a tray of massive cinnamon buns dripping with cream cheese icing. She glanced at Debbie and delivered the plates without further incident. Once the elderly couple dug into the cinnamon buns, Annie met Debbie's gaze for the briefest moment before offering a sheepish grin.

Debbie winked at Annie before turning to Janet. She lowered her voice. "I'm not so sure we can draw conclusions yet. But maybe they were stationed together. Until we learn more, we can't really assume anything."

"Okay. Fair point. But we do have a link between Samuel Lapp and Richard Brown. That link is Eileen Palmer and the letter." Janet appeared deep in thought as she placed the plastic lid on her ceramic mug.

"We also know that the Lapps were angry with Eileen for the longest time, refusing to forgive her for Samuel leaving the plain life," Debbie added.

Janet wrinkled her nose. "So we have a very sullen family who shunned Samuel and whose descendants are suddenly interested in their lost uncle's correspondence."

"Not to mention, we have Becky unable to get her furniture from the Lapp family, and we have a vandal and thief—or vandals and thieves—loose in Dennison. What does Ian think about everything?" Debbie glanced back at the dining area. She had a feeling the couple with the cinnamon buns might linger longer than expected.

Janet hesitated as she cradled her travel mug. "He's as mystified as the rest of us."

"Could it be teenagers? Or is it something else? Something vindictive?" A chill swept through Debbie. She had learned to trust Ian's keen insight and logical mind. Perhaps she was overthinking this case, jumping to illogical conclusions.

Janet didn't answer.

"The Lapp men appear to be the only enemies we're aware of," Debbie added as she thought about the sullen Benjamin who had almost kicked her out of Lapp Lumber. "Their treatment of Eileen is unusually severe, especially when other Amish people forgive and show hospitality. Not every community shuns so readily."

"We can find the taint of bitterness anywhere if we look hard enough."

Janet's bold statement sent a prickle through Debbie as she considered the implications. She wasn't certain who might prove the greater threat in the end. The elusive Richard Brown, or the reticent Lapp men?

# CHAPTER NINETEEN

*A week after meeting Rafe Palmer, Eileen ran into him a second time at the post office. All of Dennison was buzzing about the dashing young man who had returned from the war. Word spread that Rafe was Mr. Carosi's nephew. He wasn't joking about his intentions to make Dennison home. While the Carosi family cooked and baked, filling the street with the most amazing scents possible, Rafe easily found work elsewhere, repairing homes and buildings and doing any odd job available.*

*She tried not to overhear the young women in the ticket booth talk about him. How they swooned over his good looks and charming demeanor! They flirted with him at every opportunity when he entered the station to repair a broken step on the platform or replace* a cracked window near the ticket booth. She, however, avoided Rafe as much as possible.

Now, as she stood in front of the gleaming silver boxes at the post office, she jabbed in the key, hoping to unlock the box and hightail it out the door before he spoke to her.

He stood a few feet from her, clutching envelopes and a rolled newspaper. Light from the transom window above the main entrance highlighted his hair. Was he waiting for her?

She forced her attention to the small box, swung it open, and snatched plenty of bills. A few odd letters stuck out, and her breath caught at the sight of stamps and addresses. But a quick scan revealed the senders to be friends of her father. Then she saw it—a large envelope resting beneath the mundane mail.

She gasped, knowing full well that brand-new sheet music lay hidden inside. She clutched the manila envelope to her chest as music filled her mind, distracting her from everything else. If she wasn't careful, she might just burst into song right there inside the post office, and that would never do.

Rafe leaned against the wall. "My, the emotions crossing your face in the span of a few seconds. I think I've witnessed startling dismay to pure joy. I'd love to know what's inside that manila envelope, but then, I can't really ask until I have your name, Miss Stationmaster. You have me at a disadvantage, since you know mine."

She carefully slid the bills—more than she cared to see—into her purse and tucked the large envelope under her arm. The arrival of her clarinet or piano sheet music was something she looked forward to, providing a temporary respite from the fear that Samuel might have died overseas. She saved her pennies and ordered new pieces as often as she could.

But she had no intention of sharing her hobbies with a stranger.

Regardless, he had a point. He'd find out her name if he didn't know it by now. More than likely, this was a ploy to further ensnare her into a conversation.

"Eileen Turner," she stated simply.

"Eileen," he said, drawing her name out as if it were a song. "A lovely name."

"You might have told me you were Alberto Carosi's nephew." She felt churlish as soon as she blurted the challenge, but she liked Alberto, and she had no desire to offend a new friend. She might tip-toe around Rafe in the days to come, but she wanted to be polite.

"I'm sorry. You're right. I haven't always received the warmest reception when people realize I'm half

Italian. My real name is Rafaello, but during the war, I shortened it to make life easier." Rafe raked a hand through his black hair. "My uncle tells me what a loyal customer you are and how you've sent many patrons to his restaurant. He'll be forever grateful."

She chuckled as she gripped the large envelope. "Do you know how hard it is to get good cannoli in Ohio? I'd have to drive to Columbus to find the nearest Italian restaurant. I have no intention of seeing him or his delightful family leave town."

Rafe sobered, but the admiration gleaming from his eyes made her heart do an odd hiccup.

"Is Alberto your only family?"

"No. My dad passed away when I was just a boy, and my mother still lives in New York, where the restaurants serve decent Sicilian. One day I'll talk her into moving here, as soon as I save enough money to buy a home."

"Your mother is fortunate to have someone care for her." How well she understood wanting to take care of a family member. Papa needed her more than ever. This morning he had left eggs and hash browns burning on the stove, filling the house with the odor of scorched food. Not to mention he ruined the frying pan.

Although she admired Rafe's determination to care for family, the idea of him remaining in town made her stomach dance a jitterbug. She stepped toward the door, somewhat relieved when an older man entered the post office and shuffled to the end of the room housing the mailboxes.

"Good day, Mr. Palmer," she said as she brushed past him.

"Still not going to tell me what's in the big envelope?" he teased as he glanced at the mysterious package beneath her arm.

"Let's just say it's something I look forward to every month."

With a winsome smile, he tipped his hat in her direction. "At least I know where I can find you on the fifteenth."

As she left the post office, she couldn't help but think she had just issued a challenge to Rafe Palmer.

A week later, steam rose from the hood of her rusted 1933 Plymouth. Eileen hit the steering wheel with her palms and groaned. She checked her rearview mirror for the hundredth time. The descending sun threatened evening within the hour. The empty road offered no chance of rescue. Soon she would be left alone in the dark. She grabbed her purse and hopped out of the car.

She had been waiting for nearly thirty minutes. Help wasn't coming. She'd never be able to fix the radiator, or whatever it was that had finally snapped beneath the dented hood.

Why had she gone to the gospel concert in New Philly, a town ten miles from Dennison? Although the message and music had been nourishment for her soul, now she had only two choices. Wait for someone to come along and pick her up or walk the remaining three miles home. In the dark. She shivered in her thin cotton dress. She returned to the car, retrieved her cardigan, and shoved her arms into the delicate sleeves. She followed the white line painted on the side of the road to guide drivers during blackout restrictions, and before she'd gone more than a half mile, a rumble echoed in the distance.

She moved farther to the side of the highway, forcing herself not to break into a panicked run. Hopefully, she wouldn't encounter someone unsavory. A more troubling thought made her scurry faster. If Papa woke up in the night with that wretched ache in his leg, he would need her. She had left him at home with a friend, but now she would be late, so very late, in arriving home.

The car rolled to a stop, sputtering like it was choking on trail dust. She shielded her eyes, her *thoughts whirling as she tried to see the driver. A car window squealed as the glass slid down, overriding the pounding in her ears.*

*"Are you lost, Eileen Turner?" A deep voice resonated above the sound of the engine.*

*Of all the times to encounter Rafe Palmer.*

*"No," she said as she kept walking, more embarrassed than she could remember. "I know where I'm headed, thank you."*

*"Was that your car I passed back there?"*

*She took another step, wincing as her shoes pinched. "Sadly, yes. I couldn't get it to go another inch." Possibly true of her shoes at the moment too.*

*"Come on, Eileen, my carriage is your carriage. It won't turn into a pumpkin at midnight. Thank goodness I had to run errands in New Philly for my cousin, or you'd be stranded." He watched her while keeping one hand on the wheel as the car slowly inched forward. A mischievous grin brought twin dimples to his cheeks. "Would you like a ride home?"*

*She stopped at the edge of the paved road and straightened to her full height with her fists propped on her hips, fully intending to tease him in return despite her frustration at the situation. "I do not get in the cars of strange men, especially after dark. Good night, Master Sergeant."*

Harry had shared the rank a few weeks ago, after prying it out of Rafe. Master Gunnery Sergeant. No small feat, indeed.

Rafe blew out a breath and saluted. "Are we being formal again? We've already met, as I'm sure you remember. Rafe will do just fine. But, as you wish, Miss Stationmaster. It's a long way back to Dennison, and I would hate to see you walk all that way in the dark. Alone." The jesting tone turned sober. "Please, Eileen. I'll play the radio. I promise I'll behave."

"I bet you don't even have a working radio in that car," she growled, fully aware of how her new leather shoes had rubbed the back of her heels raw. She wasn't sure what chafed more, not planning for a car tune-up, or accepting a ride with a well-known flirt.

"Okay. I'll sing for you, my lady."

That made her smile, and he must have sensed the change in her mood despite the darkness. He turned off the engine, hopped out of the car, and dashed over to open the door on the passenger side. With a flourish, he bowed and held out a welcoming hand. "Your chariot awaits, mademoiselle."

"Stationmaster, mademoiselle, my lady. You sure know how to throw around the titles, don't you?"

"Well, I could try sweetheart, but I'm a little scared of your right hook."

*She laughed as she eased onto the seat. He winked at her and shut the door, and then he jogged around the car to slip into the driver's seat before turning the key in the ignition. The car purred to life.*

*And sure enough, he had music for her, with a voice that would have made Frank Sinatra swoon with jealousy. Rafe started with something humorous. She found herself singing along to "If You Stub Your Toe on the Moon."*

*She laughed just as a faint but full moon, caught in the last glimmer of the fading sunset, crested above the trees. Music always lifted her spirits. She snuck a glance at the man beside her. It hit her how handsome he was, especially with his hair cut short, highlighting his square jaw. Had she ever seen him without a saucy gleam in his eyes? Or did he do that for all the ladies in town?*

*He sang heartily while driving the car as if it were a natural extension of himself. As twilight deepened, strange blinking eyes peered from the safety of the thicket lining the road. Startled birds flew away, and a terrified rodent raced to safety. Ahead, a black buggy suddenly emerged from the shadows, rattling down the road.*

*"Look out!" she blurted, her voice unnaturally loud and strained. Thanks to the nationwide effort to turn off all lights in towns and cities, driving without*

headlights was infinitely harder and mostly to be avoided at night.

"I see it," he said as he eased up on the gas and carefully steered to the left side of the road, giving the Amish buggy a wide berth. She froze, yet she released a strangled sound, and all she could see was Samuel reaching for her and pulling her close to his chest. How that memory hurt, even years later.

"Eileen, are you okay?" Rafe's question snapped her back to the present.

She smoothed her skirt with trembling fingers. Would she ever forget Samuel and finally move on with her life? "I...uh, yes. I'm fine."

Rafe said nothing more, but he shot her a puzzled look. She swallowed hard, forcing her attention away from the side mirror, which provided a faint glimpse of a trotting horse and buggy hiding the occupant inside.

"Please, Rafe, would you keep singing?"

"For you? Yes."

He sang again. This time low and sweet, choosing gospel songs that soothed her racing pulse. His rich voice wrapped around her like a worn but comfortable quilt. She settled back into the seat, her head cradled by the headrest as the trees blurred on either side, leaving her past further and further behind. And before she knew it, she fell asleep.

She felt a hand on her shoulder. Then her cheek.

"Eileen. Princess. Time to wake up. As much as I'm willing to carry you into your castle, I don't want the neighbors gossiping."

Her eyes fluttered open, and there was Rafe, close enough to kiss as he leaned over her. There was no teasing glint in his expression. In fact, quite the opposite.

"Can I walk you to the door?" His voice thickened. "And then I'll go right home once I've made certain you're safe inside your house."

She nodded, unable to speak. The day had taken more out of her than she realized. He opened the car door for her and offered her his hand. She took it, rising to stand on unstable feet. Suddenly, her knees felt weak.

"Thank you for rescuing me," she said. "I'm grateful it was you out there, and not someone else."

His hand, which still held hers, tightened before letting go.

"I'll gladly be there for you whenever you need me."

No flirting. No winking. Just a simple admission that crept into the lonely places of her heart. He stopped midway on her sidewalk, waiting as promised, until she fished her key out of her purse. Offering him a smile and a murmured good night, she unlocked the door before entering a quiet house.

The last thought she had as she watched the car pull away was how much she missed his singing.

# CHAPTER TWENTY

Lapp Lumber appeared quiet on Thursday afternoon when Debbie opened the front door. The bell jingled, but no one greeted her at the long counter where a familiar carbon pad and pen waited. Instead, the faint but acrid scent of smoke wafted on the summer breeze and into the storefront.

"Hello?" Janet called out from behind Debbie.

Debbie waited at the counter. She noticed a small bell and hit it with her palm, the ding slightly louder than the tinkling bells above the doorway. No one came. At least the gorgeous cabinet remained pushed against the wall, just as perfect as she remembered.

"Do you think it would be okay to look around for someone to help us?" she asked.

Janet glanced at the large wooden clock with brass numerals on the wall. "I hope so. I don't want supper to be too late tonight."

"I'll be the one to enter the dangerous cave," Debbie joked, but a sliver of frustration brought an edge to her voice. "You stay put."

She moved past shelves stocked with wood trim, floorboards, nails of every size imaginable, and other building necessities. At the back, a screen door stood open to the elements, allowing a warm breeze to stir instead of blasts of icy air-conditioning.

Already she felt sticky and hot with the August humidity. A bead of sweat dripped between her shoulder blades. The scent of smoke grew much stronger as she stepped into the lumberyard where the Lapp men sawed wood. Although they didn't use electricity, the way a non-Amish business would, they weren't opposed to utilizing diesel engines. Debbie had heard rumors that the new bishop wasn't as strict as his predecessors.

Her steps made no sound on the sturdy porch, which ran down the length of the lumberyard. The Lapps were clearly prosperous, judging by the care of the buildings and grounds and the amount of wood, supplies, and an additional steel-covered building with white trim to Debbie's right. Cheerful daisies grew along the side of the workshop, perhaps the work of Hannah.

Debbie removed her sunglasses and hooked them into her shirt pocket. Her gaze returned to the center of the lumberyard, where a blackened barrel smoked as a young Amish man dumped a cloth sack full of papers into it. He didn't notice her standing beneath the shadowed awning. No one else appeared to be in the yard, although the sounds of hammers striking and men's voices, loud and clear, echoed from the workshop.

The fire crackled and snapped, devouring the contents. After pushing up his hat, the young man wiped his flushed brow with the back of his hand. With a sickening feeling, Debbie recognized Benjamin Lapp. His face hardened like granite as he stared into the hungry flames. He clutched a vintage flour sack in his hand, the kind used to make dresses during the Great Depression.

"Hello there," Debbie called out as she entered the yard.

Benjamin jumped, his frosty blue gaze narrowing as he saw her approach.

"This area is closed to visitors. We do not do tours here. It is not safe, and I will need you to go back to where you came from."

"I came to purchase a cabinet, and no one is at the front counter."

He pursed his lips before tossing the flour sack into the barrel. "I will write a receipt and load it for you."

Without another word, he stomped up the steps to the porch, brushing past Debbie while the scent of smoke clung to his worn blue shirt and pants.

Okay. Perhaps grumpiness made up Benjamin Lapp's permanent mood.

She followed him into the front section of the store. "Is Hannah around? My friend would love to talk baking with her, if she's available."

He didn't break stride. His boots clomped heavily on the hardwood floor. "Ja, she is in the workshop, helping Daed."

He eyed Janet and quoted a slightly reduced price than Hannah had days prior.

Janet pulled a wad of cash from her wallet and handed it to him. "Can you deliver it? Even if we lower the rear seats in my car, I'm not sure we'd be able to fit it in. I'd hate to scratch my car or the cabinet."

"Ja, I think we can deliver it. Let me check my schedule." He opened a notebook and flipped through the pages.

Debbie glanced down and realized her sunglasses were missing. Catching Janet's gaze, she jerked her head toward the rear entrance. "I must have dropped my sunglasses in the yard. I'll be only a second."

Benjamin scowled, his glare transforming his handsome face into something that made a shiver skip down her spine. "No one is allowed out there without supervision."

"I'm sure I'll find them on the deck. I'd hate to lose this pair." Debbie gave him an extra sweet smile.

Janet raised her eyebrows as Debbie inched backward, and then she distracted Benjamin with several rapid-fire questions about the craftsmanship of the woodwork.

"So do you use a diesel engine to cut the wood? How do you sand the boards?" Debbie heard Janet ask.

Debbie kept her backward walk as Benjamin's attention refocused on Janet. Seeing her opportunity, she practically melted away, rushing toward the yard. Could she retrieve the sunglasses and check the contents of the burn barrel without Benjamin seeing?

An anguished cry resounded and, there, in the center of the yard, Hannah stood by the burning bin, trying to rescue the cloth sack with a blackened stick.

Debbie rushed to the young woman, her heart pounding at the sight. "Hannah, are you burned?"

Hannah raised her reddened eyes from the fire, and the look of grief made Debbie's chest ache. "Ne. I am not hurt. The fire is hot, so do not get too close." She raised a sooty fist, covering her mouth as a cough racked her thin frame. All at once, the wind shifted direction, blowing smoke into Debbie's face and forcing her to turn aside as her eyes watered. The gusts of air renewed the flames with a roar.

With another broken cry, Hannah tried again with the stick, poking the smoldering collection of papers. The wind caught a portion of one, swirling it higher amid glowing embers until it sank onto the debris, curling into ash. But not before Debbie noted a section of handwriting on the scorched paper.

Her breath froze when she read the return address of what remained of a ruined envelope.

*Richard Brown*

*La Jolla Farms, California*

Richard Brown had contacted the Lapps? Why had Benjamin burned his letter?

With a low moan, Hannah dropped the stick into the barrel, her shoulders slumped in defeat as she covered her face with her hands.

Debbie tentatively reached out a hand to pat the young woman on the shoulder. "I'm so sorry for whatever you lost. Is there anything I can do to help?"

Hannah inhaled sharply before coughing a second time. "Ne." Her voice roughened. "My bruder likes to clean house. He did not think to ask me if I would like to keep a few mementos. He has never been one to hold on to anything sentimental or anything frivolous."

"He sounds very practical," Debbie said lamely. More than anything, she wanted to grab a second stick and poke around the ashy depths of the barrel to discover or rescue what else might lie within the embers, but she also didn't want to leave Hannah's side, especially when the young woman was so grieved.

Hannah wiped her eyes with the edge of her apron, leaving a trace of soot streaked across her reddened nose. "Ja, Benjamin is certainly practical, just like my daed. Oh well, no use in crying over spilt milk, as my *dawdi* used to say." She smiled before squaring her shoulders. "What brings you to Lapp Lumber?"

"We bought one of your cabinets for the café. I think it will be the perfect accent piece. Guests can view antiques and a little bit of the station's history."

"I am thrilled you returned to purchase it. I was not certain I would ever see you again after my bruder's earlier behavior. Both Daed and I agreed our customers must come first." She leaned forward and said softly, "I've asked my daed to review your friend Becky's order. He told me he would contact her a second time and discuss it further. I am certain we can come to a reasonable agreement. I have pulled all the previous records, searching for the furniture your friend said she purchased. So far, I have not found the additional items, but I will keep hunting."

Debbie spotted her glasses lying on the gravel. She retrieved them, moaning at the new scratch on one of the lenses. "Wonderful news. I'm certain Becky will appreciate your efforts."

"*Ach,* your poor sunglasses." Hannah reached into the pocket of her dress and took out a handkerchief. "Would this help remove some of the dust? I hope you will not need a new pair."

Debbie grinned, forgoing the hem of her shirt for the cotton handkerchief. She carefully wiped the sunglasses, removing the smudges. "It's no problem. I'm glad I ran into you."

"Me too. I owe you a recipe, do I not? We have been so busy at the lumberyard, I have not mailed it, and Benjamin does not like it when I drive the buggy on my own. Do you have time to come to the house while I write something out for your friend? My maam told me the kuchen recipe goes back four generations."

Why wouldn't Benjamin let Hannah drive the buggy by herself? Debbie saw Amish women driving alone every day. Was the

Lapp family especially strict, even beyond the Ordnung? Her nerves tingled again when she remembered Benjamin's rudeness. She highly doubted he had learned the lesson his father intended.

She put her sunglasses on top of her head. "I'd love the kuchen recipe. Let me tell Janet, and we'll come together. Your brother is finishing up the order."

Hannah's expression dimmed. "You are likely too busy to visit, especially if you need to leave soon."

"Nonsense. We'd love to visit with you if your family doesn't mind."

Hannah sucked in another deep breath. Uncertainty flickered in her eyes, but she nodded once, as if deciding. "Ja, I would like a visit. I will wait right here while you finish your business with Benjamin."

By the time Debbie rejoined Janet, Benjamin had already departed. Of course, Janet didn't need to be asked twice about receiving a special family recipe handed down through the generations.

Hannah waited for them, her shy demeanor so winsome after Benjamin's sullenness. The young woman led them through the lumberyard to a back entrance where a gated fence kept visitors from wandering onto the property.

Beyond a copse of rustling trees, an enormous white house with a wraparound porch spread across a lawn dotted with wildflowers.

A second winding entrance, one of gravel, allowed private access to the family's residence. Beside the house, a small corral contained a pair of horses. A black buggy was parked nearby.

Debbie stopped, exclaiming over the horses as they flicked flies away with their tails. What she really wanted to see was the back end of the buggy. As she drifted past the corral, she spied an unbroken shiny reflector. Had Benjamin changed it recently?

Hannah climbed the steps and opened the screen door, gesturing for Janet and Debbie to enter. The house smelled of fresh baked apples and cinnamon. Inside, the space seemed luxuriously large, if austere. Braided rag rugs covered the wide-planked floor. Green curtains framed sparkling clean windows. A pair of rocking chairs was positioned in front of a towering stone fireplace with an enormous mantel of rugged wood. Next to the kitchen, a magnificent oak table brought an appreciative gasp from Janet.

"I'm assuming your father or brother made this beautiful furniture," Debbie said as she ran a finger across the smooth grain of the dining room table large enough to seat twelve.

Hannah nodded as she opened one of the kitchen cupboards and pulled out a recipe box. "Some of the furniture was made by my dawdi, Jacob. He built the dining room table. Daed and Benjamin made the rocking chairs. The house has furniture four generations old. We cherish it all the more because we know the stories behind the pieces."

A small table, decorated with laced fretwork unlike anything Debbie had ever seen, sat tucked next to one of the rocking chairs. The two-toned wood seemed extravagant when compared to the other furniture. She felt there was a story connected to this piece. "Who made this side table? It has a certain artistic flair."

"Jacob's bruder, Samuel, made that one."

"Samuel Lapp?" Janet asked quietly.

Hannah skimmed through the recipes, her gaze trained on the white cards. "Ja. I have been told no one could carve like him. He etched animals and flowers into the wood like it was nothing more than butter. Jacob did not like to talk much about his bruder, but he did say that Samuel was in high demand for his lacy woodwork. People from Kentucky, West Virginia, and even farther would beg for custom furniture from Samuel. Truthfully, Jacob was just as good with the wood. He had a simpler style, that is all."

Debbie glanced at Janet. She didn't want to put too much pressure on Hannah. But the more Hannah shared, the more jealous her grandfather Jacob appeared.

"Few can carve with that degree of skill."

Hannah frowned as she pulled out a recipe card. "Ja, as I understand it, the bishop back then thought Samuel's furniture prideful. Our current bishop does not pay much heed to such things. However, current styles have changed. People want the plain pieces, so my daed and bruder are more popular than ever."

"Did Jacob ever hear from Samuel after he left for the war?"

"Ja, he did. But the bruders remained on hard terms. Jacob wanted nothing to do with Samuel."

"Do you have copies of Samuel's letters from the war?"

Hannah's fingers hovered over the recipe cards. "Ne, the letters are lost forever, I am afraid." A quiver of her bottom lip suggested tears held at bay.

The image of a blackened barrel filled Debbie's mind as she recalled Benjamin dumping papers into the hungry flames.

"I am sorry." Hannah pushed the recipe box aside. "I think the recipe must be in the attic. Will you give me a moment to find it? I have coffee, if you would like. Or lemonade."

"Take your time." Janet smiled as she sat in a rocking chair. "Lemonade sounds perfect on a hot day."

Hannah pulled glasses from a cupboard and went out to the porch. When she returned, she held a pitcher of lemonade. "We have an icebox out there," she said as she handed a full glass to Debbie. "I made the lemonade earlier for lunch, just the way daed likes it."

Debbie tasted a perfect blend of tart and sweet as refreshing as she had hoped. Hannah gave a glass to Janet before climbing a wide staircase and disappearing from sight.

"I think I need a rocking chair." Janet sighed. "I wonder what Ian would say if I brought one home tonight."

"How would you get it there? Strap it to the car roof with a bit of rope and a few prayers?" Debbie teased.

"Not on your life. I've got enough explaining to do with the scratches to the bumper and rock chips in the windshield. I'm always the one who gets dinged when I drive, never him. Maybe he could borrow a pickup truck and buy a pair for us."

Debbie smiled, but her attention was honed on Hannah's movements upstairs. Now that they had a moment of privacy, she moved away from the kitchen cupboards.

"Janet," she whispered, "I caught Benjamin burning papers when we first arrived. You won't believe what I saw in his barrel.

An envelope addressed by our Richard Brown all the way from California!"

Janet's eyes widened. She opened her mouth to answer when a door slammed with a rattle.

"What are you doing in my kitchen?" a man's voice boomed.

Debbie whirled to see Daniel Lapp tugging his straw hat from his head, his jaw set in a hard line.

# CHAPTER TWENTY-ONE

O h dear," Debbie heard Janet mutter from the rocking chair. She straightened when another man entered the kitchen, letting the screen door bang behind him.

"You!" Benjamin cried as he stumbled on the braided rag rug at the entrance.

Daniel held his hat, twisting it over and over in his massive hands. "Forgive us. I—I am not used to guests, nor is my son." He glanced at Debbie then Janet. "To what do I owe the pleasure of this surprise?"

*He's not used to uninvited guests wandering through the lumber-yard and kitchen, no doubt*, Debbie thought. She smiled at him. "I hope you don't mind, but Hannah invited us inside to discuss kuchen recipes."

"We also came to purchase one of your lovely cabinets," Janet said as she rose from the rocking chair. "Thanks to Benjamin, I've learned a little more about Amish woodworking."

Benjamin scowled as he thumbed his suspenders.

"I assume Hannah invited you for coffee? Where is she?" Daniel cast a gaze toward the wide staircase.

"Delicious lemonade." Debbie raised her glass. "Hannah is upstairs hunting for her famous kuchen recipe."

"Ah." Daniel licked his lips. "Lemonade sounds wunderbaar after a hot afternoon of work." He hung his hat on a hook near the door, found a glass, and poured the lemonade. Benjamin folded his arms across his chest, refusing the refreshing drink.

Debbie reached for her bag, offering a prayer at the same time. "Actually, we have something for you, sent with Eileen Palmer's blessing. She said we could let you read Samuel's letter. Would you like to see it?"

She was thankful she hadn't delivered the letter to Benjamin. Would he have immediately dumped it into the fire?

Daniel wiped his mouth and set the glass on the counter. "Ja, please tell Mrs. Palmer her offer is very kind."

Earlier in the day, Debbie had placed the letter in a file folder. She handed the folder to Daniel.

He pulled a pair of wire-rimmed glasses out of his shirt pocket and removed the letter. His eyes darted back and forth as he read it. At last, he placed the letter on the counter. Debbie noted the quiver in his sturdy fingers.

"Danki," he said thickly. "I remember my grossmammi praying for Samuel. She would have liked to have read this and known where Samuel was stationed. She missed him terribly, right until the day of her passing. Her last words were of her lost son and her prayer that the family might be reunited again one day."

The admission touched Debbie's heart, thawing it at the edges. Perhaps not everyone had wanted Samuel shunned as she first assumed. "I had a praying grandmother. I'll never forget how her prayers encouraged me."

A sympathetic smile lifted the corner of Daniel's mouth.

"A man named Richard Brown dropped Samuel's letter at the train station. Have you received any contact from him?"

The room grew silent. Daniel opened his mouth and snapped it shut and then suddenly clutched his chest with one hand. "Ach—" Agony contorted his features into a grimace as he planted the other palm on the kitchen counter.

"Daed! Sit down, please." Benjamin rushed to his father's side, placed an arm around the older man's waist, and led him to the empty rocking chair beside the fireplace.

Debbie shot a glance at Janet. Had her question triggered chest pains in Daniel? Fear he might be having a heart attack made her feel nauseated. "We have our car. Can we take you to the nearest clinic?"

Daniel's face turned a sickly hue. A gurgle escaped him as he rubbed his chest. He sounded out of breath, as if he had a run a marathon. "Ja, please. It has been a long day with many customers."

"Do not talk," Benjamin ordered as he lingered near the rocking chair.

"I found the recipe! It was hiding beneath a few quilts." Footsteps pounded down the stairs. Hannah held an index card in her hands, her triumphant smile disappearing when she saw her father slumped in the rocking chair.

"Daed! Not again," she cried as she rushed to her father.

Debbie grimaced as her mind raced with potential outcomes, none of them good. "Janet, will you call the Uhrichsville ER? If we take our car, we could be there much sooner than the ambulance. We'll lose precious time if we wait for it."

"I think we can make room for everyone in the car," Janet said as she moved toward the door with her phone in her hand. "I'll call the ER now and see if they can prepare for us."

Hannah hugged herself tightly while Benjamin remained close to his father.

The young man's eyes watered as he squeezed his father's shoulder. Debbie feared to know what he might be thinking. Surely Benjamin must blame his father's condition on her and Janet. In her effort to find answers for Eileen, someone got hurt. The last thing she wanted to do was add to this family's pain.

"Just breathe, Daed. It will be okay. I promise." Benjamin patted his father's back. Daniel's nostrils flared, but his breathing remained quick and shallow, his chest rising and falling more rapidly than Debbie cared to see.

She couldn't help but wonder about Benjamin's earlier burning of an assortment of papers. The Lapps kept their secrets close. Too close. Had Benjamin burned letters, or something of importance to the family? His actions felt sneaky.

And why did the name Richard Brown create such a terrible reaction?

The emergency room remained blissfully peaceful on a Thursday evening, the waiting room empty at suppertime. The only sounds came from a flat-screen television mounted to the wall, blaring a game show. Debbie paced back and forth in the waiting room while Hannah sat in a chair, her head bowed. Plum vinyl-covered chairs and pastel artwork attempted to make the space more soothing. Debbie couldn't relax, and from the looks of her fidgeting, neither could Hannah. A coffee dispenser offered tepid coffee in minuscule foam cups.

Janet had stepped outside the ER to call Ian. Through the sliding glass doors, Debbie watched her friend pace on the sidewalk, her features pinched with worry.

Thanks to Janet's quick phone call, the nurses were ready to assist Daniel to a bed as soon as Janet pulled up to the ER entrance. The head ER nurse arranged for Daniel to be admitted for further assessment. At the moment, he was changing into a hospital gown. The nurse promised to bring Hannah along for the testing as soon as her father finished dressing. Benjamin had insisted on staying with his father in the room.

Hannah wiped her eyes with a tissue. "Do you think my daed will be okay?"

Debbie's heart filled with sympathy. "I hope so. The physician on call has ordered an EKG and a chest X-ray to look for any hidden problems. The phlebotomist will bring a cart to the room and draw blood."

The young woman sniffled as she balled the tissue and threw it into the nearby trash can. She glanced at Debbie. "For once, I am grateful to have had a car nearby and not the buggy. A horse can only go so fast."

"You mentioned your brother doesn't like you driving."

Hannah snatched another tissue and blew her nose. "He is afraid for my safety if I leave on my own. He thinks some cute Englischer boy will try to pick me up and whisk me far away. Of course I tell him that if I run into trouble, I will drive home as fast as I can. That does not make Benjamin feel very assured. I had an accident the last time I drove the buggy, breaking a wheel. Since then, he insists on driving."

"Tell your brother he doesn't get a say in your driving or racing," Debbie said with a hint of smile. To her surprise, Hannah chuckled, her posture relaxing.

"Has your father been ill before this incident?"

"Ja," Hannah said as she dabbed at her eyes and nose. "He tries to hide it, of course. But he gets these spells when he cannot breathe and his chest aches something fierce. The more stress he feels, the worse it is. Especially ever since…ever since we've been getting letters."

"From Richard Brown?"

Hannah reached for another tissue from the box, her eyes widening at the mention of the mysterious man. "Ja, Richard Brown."

"Who is he, and what does he want with your family?"

Hannah lowered her voice to a whisper. "He says he knew my great-uncle Samuel. And he will tell us what happened to Samuel if we will meet with him in private to talk. That is all I know about Richard. I was not allowed to read the letter, mind you. After my daed got it about two months ago, he has not slept well at night, nor my bruder. They will not tell me anything more, but whoever this Richard is, he is tearing my family apart at the seams."

# CHAPTER TWENTY-TWO

*Dennison, Ohio*
*July 1946*

*The July sun simmered, promising a sweltering day more suited for ducking into a pond than shopping on Main Street, where everything baked on the pavement. Eileen adjusted her hat, pulling the straw brim lower to block the brilliant rays. Despite the beauty of the afternoon, a bittersweetness tugged at her heart. She glanced at the watch pinned to her dress. Her lunch errands, saved for between work shifts at the station, left her out of breath and out of sorts.*

*She clasped under her arm what would likely be her last order of sheet music. Money was increasingly in short supply, while her cares at home mushroomed. Her shoulders slumped as she walked down Main Street, away from the post office. None of the cheerful storefronts, including the Revco drugstore or Buona Vita's bright red awning jutting from the brick facade, could rouse her flagging spirits.*

*Leaving the house for work this morning had proven to be quite a battle. Papa wanted strawberry shortcake for breakfast, of all things. She didn't have any of the right ingredients, nor did she have an hour to spare to make something that elaborate for him to eat, especially when her work at the train station waited.*

*Dorothy, Papa's caretaker, had also shared exciting news, but it put Eileen in a dilemma. Dorothy was expecting a baby and, as a result, would no longer be available to watch him during the long days.*

*Eileen didn't want to think about leaving the train station, but how could she remain when she might not be able to find help for Papa?*

Make a way, Lord. Show me what I need to do in this situation.

*The door to the Revco drugstore swung open, and Rafe stepped outside, gripping a toolbox in his hand. He froze on the sidewalk when he saw her approach.*

*"Good morning, Mr. Palmer." Somehow, it was easier for her when she kept things formal with him, especially since that fateful car ride from New Philly. Regardless of her resolve to remain cool, her pulse picked up a notch.*

Rafe wouldn't let her pass so easily.

"It's music, isn't it?" He nodded toward the package pinned beneath Eileen's arm as she walked past the window displays.

She glanced down at the thick package. Records would be nicer but, of course, more expensive. She couldn't afford a record player anytime soon. She released a sigh of resignation when he set the paint-splattered toolbox on the pavement as if he intended to have a lengthy conversation.

She nodded. "It's my monthly shipment of piano and clarinet scores."

"You play both instruments?"

The delight in his voice brought a delicious shiver to her.

"Mostly the clarinet," she said.

He peered intently at her from beneath an unruly shock of black hair. "Then why the sad face? Normally when I see you leave the post office, you've got a bounce in your step."

How much could she explain of her situation without revealing anything too personal? She didn't want Rafe's pity, but neither could she pretend her life was normal.

She infused a lightness into her tone, even though her throat tightened. "I'm not sure I can keep up with my hobby. Duty and all. But it was fun while it lasted."

He arched his eyebrow. "Why does duty have to interfere with pursuing a dash of fun?"

"We don't all have the freedom to do as we please." The words stumbled out of her more crossly than she intended. Perhaps she wasn't being entirely fair. She had never met a man who worked as hard as Rafe. However, his insistence on thoroughly enjoying life grated on her. Or, if she was honest, challenged her, and she didn't like it at all.

"Life is meant to be savored. It can't be all work and duty. Everyone needs something to look forward to."

She shut her eyes briefly, the cares of the station and Papa weighing on her. How could she possibly break free from such concerns? Had she lost sight of what it meant to truly live beyond these quick trips to the post office for music?

"If that's your last shipment of sheet music, I hope you ordered something good," he said after a long pause.

"The Anderson Sisters. 'A Collection of Tropical Songs.' Considering the weather we're having, I thought it appropriate." She hugged the envelope closer. Somehow, the music always transported her to another place and time, and as the sisters' notes soared on the pages,

Eileen could imagine an island retreat, far from the cares and worries that plagued her. Sometimes she sang along when she played the piano, and other times, she pulled out her clarinet to play the tunes.

"Nice choice," he said with a smile. Then he took a step closer. "I bet you have the prettiest singing voice, Eileen. I hope one day I get to hear it. And that clarinet of yours." His voice was as warm as maple syrup on pancakes.

For once, she was completely speechless. And then, when she pivoted to go, her ankle turned. She lurched and felt his hand catch her. The contact was brief, his fingers strong and curled about her elbow. But it felt like an eternity before he blinked and finally let go of her arm.

After a murmured goodbye, she fled Main Street, her hand pressed against her cheek.

# CHAPTER TWENTY-THREE

It was well past nine thirty on Thursday night when Debbie unlocked her front door. Exhaustion flooded her as she flipped on the light switch in the hall. The hospital emergency and all that happened there clung to her. She rubbed her eyes, grateful to be finally home after a long day of work, buying a cabinet, *and* a stressful ER visit. The local Amish bishop had kindly offered to house Hannah and Benjamin, should the need arise for Daniel to stay at the hospital overnight. In the end, the EKG and X-rays revealed nothing abnormal for the older man. Blood work too.

"The ER doctor said it was a panic attack," Hannah had whispered to Debbie after a conference with the on-call physician. Debbie had passed the time with Hannah, thumbing through dated fashion and home decor magazines, offering a continual stream of silent prayers for the Lapp family.

Hannah picked up a magazine on the table, but she didn't open it. "Daed gets so worked up that he cannot breathe, and then he gets dizzy. I guess that is why his chest hurts so much. The doctor offered to keep him overnight to watch, but otherwise, his heart is as healthy as our horse Mindy."

Relieved to hear Daniel would likely be hale enough to return home the same day, Debbie had offered to drive the family back to the farmhouse. However, Benjamin would have none of it.

"You have done enough to my family," he had said when no one else was near in the ER waiting room. "I want no more visits or purchases or requests for recipes. Do you understand me?"

She understood perfectly. It was just what the family had done to Eileen almost eighty years ago.

"I think we could help each other, Benjamin. We both want answers from Richard. Why don't we work together?"

"Ne. No good can come from fraternizing with an Englischer. That is all I need to know." Benjamin's firm answer left no room for Debbie to argue. She couldn't help but worry about the Lapp family, particularly Hannah, whose reddened eyes and nose showed more tears.

Bless Pastor Nick's heart. He volunteered to drive the Lapps home despite a long day of serving. When Debbie had snuck a peek at Benjamin just before leaving the hospital, the icy facade had melted, and he discreetly wiped away a tear.

She kicked one sneaker off, and then the next, too tired to straighten her shoes by the doorway. The shadowed hallway appeared unusually forbidding. Her phone rang.

She looked at the screen and saw Greg's name.

For a moment, she debated muting the ringtone. She couldn't remember feeling so tired or so discouraged. Instead, she tapped the answer icon.

"Hi, Debbie." Greg's deep voice brought a measure of comfort.

"Hi," she answered.

"Sorry to bother you so late. I just ran into Janet. She said you were both gone all afternoon and evening. Have you had supper yet?"

She pressed the phone against her ear, now glad for the company when the house felt so empty and spooky. She had debated calling her mother, but it was too late —her mom usually went to bed just before nine. "Uh, no. It's been a crazy day, as I'm sure Janet shared with you."

"I just ordered fried chicken for my boys. It's bedtime, I know. But I wondered if I could bring by an extra box for you."

"You're having supper at this hour?"

He laughed. "It's been a long day of framing and drywall. My boys and I were planning to get a late supper. The gas station makes some of the best fried chicken I've ever tasted. I'd be happy to share. I'll even add an order of potato wedges, if you'd like."

Her stomach growled loudly. "Oh Greg, that would be amazing. Between the café and trying to help Eileen, I haven't had a chance to stock my fridge. I'll gladly pay you."

"It's okay, Debbie. What are friends for? Besides, consider all the times you and Janet have fed me at the café. I was going to drop off an order of chicken for her as well, but Ian had already made their supper."

Relief flooded Debbie as she moved to the living room. Greg was demonstrating a simple kindness. After she ended the call, she collapsed into the nearest chair and stretched her legs onto the matching ottoman.

Her phone vibrated, and she saw a new voice mail.

To Debbie's delight, Cheryl Miller, from the Swiss Miss in Sugarcreek, had left a detailed message, asking for a time to chat about the Amish enlisted man, Frank Raber. It was too late to return a call, especially since Cheryl had small children tucked in bed. Debbie would try to call in the morning.

She leaned her head against the club chair and was nearly asleep when her doorbell chimed.

She bolted upright. Outside the living room window, a pair of headlights cast a wide beam into her living room. She answered the door. Greg held up a large paper bag and a bottle of soda. Coming from a work site, he wore rugged, dark-rinse jeans and a black T-shirt splattered with white paint. Time spent outside was evident in his deep tan and reddened nose. Behind him, his red construction truck idled, and his dog, Hammer, a black-and-white border collie, whined from the partially opened window. Both Jaxon and Julian waited in the truck. Debbie waved at them, and Julian raised his hand in greeting.

"I bring sustenance." Greg handed the bag and the bottle to her. Her stomach growled a second time when she smelled the chicken. Hammer yipped from the truck, his enormous tongue hanging out of a big doggie grin.

"Settle down, Hammer. I saved you some treats." Greg laughed as he consoled his dog.

"Greg, this is…" She cleared her throat. "This is one of the nicest things anyone has done for me, other than Janet's experimental baking and coffee, of course."

"Rough day, I gather."

"The worst."

Because the boys were waiting, she didn't invite him into her home, and he seemed content to stay within the circle of her well-lit porch. "We went to visit the Lapp family. We thought Daniel had a heart attack, but it turned out he had a panic attack."

Greg's brows lowered. "What caused it?"

"I saw an envelope burning in their barrel, addressed from our mysterious Richard Brown, who has also visited the town library searching for articles written by the Unnamed Soldier. When I asked about Richard, Daniel paled and grabbed his chest. I can't imagine a family having so many secrets. Not even Hannah understands fully what's happening. But she wants it to end."

"I think you need to sit down with Ian and discuss it further. Maybe it's time to get his advice." Greg jammed his hands into his pockets. "What if Richard Brown is stalking or harassing the Lapps?"

Debbie paused, disturbed by the allegation. Was Richard toying with the Lapps? If so, why? "You're right. I had hoped Janet and I could get to the bottom of things, especially since Ian is so busy these days. I hate to bug him."

"That's the benefit of living in a small town. We're all here for each other. You'll never burden him. Or me." Greg yawned suddenly, triggering the same reaction in her.

"You must be tired, and here I am chatting," Debbie said, embarrassed to keep him.

He smiled. "No, no. I enjoy it, but you're right. I was up at five this morning, installing additional security cameras around the station. Mark helped me with the wiring, which was a boon. Now you and Janet can work in peace without worrying about strangers or anything else."

How wonderfully thoughtful of him, ensuring the safety of his friends. The warmth in her chest spread.

"We'll all feel more at ease, I'm sure."

He lightly touched her shoulder, the movement natural, but swift. "I won't keep you from your supper, Debbie. Try not to worry about Daniel and Eileen, okay? God will work out the details in His timing. He always does."

She waved as Greg returned to his truck. After he drove away, she pondered his encouraging words. She did worry—perhaps not to the same degree as Daniel and Benjamin, but she couldn't deny that this situation had her deeply troubled.

She went into the kitchen and took a plate and a cup from the cupboard. She opened the bag and pulled out a red-and-white striped box of fried chicken. The idea of crispy wings and drumsticks made her mouth water. Just as Greg promised, an order of potato wedges lay beside the chicken, along with a sealed container of coleslaw. Another package with a gold sticker made her grin. A large chocolate iced brownie promised a sweet finish to the filling meal.

"Oh, Greg," she murmured. Suddenly, eating alone in her kitchen didn't feel so lonely. She said a prayer for the Lapps and for her friends, including Greg, who had welcomed her so graciously to Dennison.

As she removed the plastic lid on the coleslaw, her focus collided with a picture of her fiancé on a shelf. Reed gazed at her, affection shining in his eyes. The memory suddenly felt as real as if it were yesterday. The small photo cased in a distressed wood frame rested against a collection of antique cookbooks which were more for display than actual use. A favorite photo. She really ought to remove it. But every time she tried, she couldn't. Her engagement ring, a simple gold band with a solitaire diamond, remained hidden within a jewelry box on her dresser. She had moved on with her life—or, at least she thought she had.

A pang in her heart chased away the warmth Greg had brought with a simple act of kindness. With a sigh, she focused on spooning the coleslaw onto her plate. She missed Reed. Really, it was too late to begin again in the relationship department. Greg had two teenagers and a thriving business. He didn't need someone like her, a woman comfortable with her single life. Content, even. Why ruin a good thing? She had made peace with her loss. She had enough occupying her days with the Whistle Stop Café.

Yet a sliver of warning stabbed her conscience. The more she dug into Eileen's mystery, the more her own past resurfaced.

# CHAPTER TWENTY-FOUR

*Dennison, Ohio*
*August 1946*

*Eileen crumpled the notice in her hand. She had a meeting in two weeks with her superior—a meeting that brought a nervous flutter to her chest. Someone had complained about her work, and now she would receive a review, her every action held under scrutiny. Was she truly at risk of losing her job?*

*For the past few years, she had kept herself tremendously busy at the station, feeling as though she was making a difference in her community. The demands of the job distracted her from thinking of the past, or the future. There was only the present needs of travelers, the shifting train schedules, and the never-ending noise of the trains—loud enough to drown out her thoughts. She couldn't imagine doing anything else.*

*She glanced up at the walls of her office, comforted by the familiar forest-green trim, the brass light, which flickered and hummed when the station was silent, and the old wooden desk and matching swivel chair. This was her home.*

*She tossed the paper into the metal trash can next to the desk, took her enormous key ring, and locked the office behind her. Her superior's voice, cold and businesslike, resonated in her mind. "We've had complaints, Eileen. Mind you, not many, but..."*

*Her supervisor wouldn't tell her the source of such complaints. She couldn't imagine anyone betraying her at the station. Of course, Mr. Oscar Ainsworth made no secret of the fact that he preferred a male stationmaster, even if he had praised her work. Besides, everyone else had complimented her past years of service. She had done the best she could—given it all she had.*

*Muted male voices echoed in the hall. Harry Franklin instructed a figure perched precariously on a ladder. The man reached out with a brush, carefully painting the trim with a steady hand. The stained glass windows had been painted black in case of a surprise enemy attack. Now that the threat had passed, those same windows had been scraped clean, bringing the colored blocks of red, blue, green, and yellow back to life.*

Little by little, the train station underwent a transformation, removing the wear and tear the war had brought.

The man on the ladder hummed beneath his breath as he dragged the brush in a straight line. An overbearing smell of oil paint and turpentine made Eileen wrinkle her nose. But the man didn't seem to care. In fact, he appeared to enjoy himself while balancing on the narrow rungs. Below him, Harry offered more advice, pointing to spots needing a second coat of paint.

Eileen looked up and saw Rafe Palmer. He had become a constant in her life. He had settled in Dennison and started a small handyman business, which had blossomed into bigger projects. He recently fixed the leaky pipe in the bank and the ruined white ceiling tiles. He hung a new door in Dorothy's cottage. Wherever he went, he charmed everyone, old and young alike.

Ever since the car ride, he had been especially careful with her, offering a tip of the hat at church or a murmured hello at the post office. She hadn't taken him up on his offer for dinner at Buona Vita. Would he invite her a second time, or had she missed her chance?

Taking a deep, shaking breath to control her emotions, she walked down the hall, her heels clattering against the floor.

"Hello, Miss Eileen." Harry beamed as she passed. "We're going to get the station looking like new again."

"That's wonderful, Harry." She tried to infuse enthusiasm into her voice and failed, apparently, since Rafe paused, his long arm still outstretched with a paintbrush. He glanced down at her, his expression hard to read.

Harry called over his shoulder. "I'll say good night, ma'am. Did I tell you Homer caught a mouse the other day?"

She shook her head. Harry and Homer had bonded at the station, and it seemed fitting that the kitten—now a full-grown cat—go to him. "He's quite the hunter. I'm glad it worked out for the both of you."

Harry waved as he left, leaving her alone with Rafe in the hall.

How could she say goodbye to the station and this life she had carved for herself? Surely Mr. Ainsworth wouldn't fire her. Tears filled her eyes. Of all the ridiculous times to cry, especially with Rafe right above her. She blinked back her tears.

"Looks like you're doing a great job," she said just as the ladder shook with his weight. He rapidly climbed down the rungs and carefully placed the paintbrush in an open bucket.

He faced her as he straightened. "Are you okay?"

He had asked her the same question once before, and she had refused to answer. She clasped her hands behind her back, thinking of the letter in the trash can.

"Yes—no." The concern in his gaze brought a stubborn ache to her throat. For once, she shared how she really felt. "No, I'm not okay. I'm to be evaluated as stationmaster in two weeks. My father needs me more than ever. I'm wondering what life will hold now that the war is over, and, well...I'm a little—"

He waited for her to continue, and so she did. "I'm scared. I love my father, and I'm grateful to take care of him, but I hate to see him fade away. I hate to—"

To lose another someone or something I love.

The tears came then, and he handed her a white linen hanky, slightly wrinkled, but clean.

"I'm sorry about the stress you're under."

She dabbed at the corner of her eyes. "It's a new season in life, I guess." Honestly, she couldn't stand any more change.

To her surprise, he touched her shoulder, the gesture comforting. His hand felt warm and solid. "What if God brings you into a better season? Leading you from winter into spring, so you can move ahead into the plan He's always had for you?"

She hid behind the handkerchief, the truth of what Rafe said settling over her. Trust Rafe to view his circumstances through the lens of joy. If she was completely honest, she wanted a taste of some of his joy too.

"You might be right. Thank you for listening." She struggled to regain her composure, her breath hitching.

He watched her with a careful expression. "I'm considered a good listener."

"With good taste in music," she mumbled. When she handed the handkerchief to him, he smiled. "Sinatra forever."

She rose to the bait. "Oh no, he has nothing on the Mills Brothers."

"Is that so? What about 'Stella by Starlight'?"

She blushed for the second time around him. Sinatra all but melted when singing of two lovers hiding beneath a starry sky, and of a girl worth everything to him.

"It's a nice song," she said. Glancing at her watch, she realized she needed to leave, or Papa wouldn't have supper. "It's late, and I've got to run. I'd like to say I'll see you around, but I'm afraid everything is about to change."

He shoved his hands in pockets. "Oh, that's debatable. There's always Buona Vita. My invitation still stands. Would you care to join me sometime?"

A smile broke free, despite the dampness on her cheeks. "I might take you up on the offer, Mr. Palmer."

Eileen opened her door on a Saturday morning. There, on the pavement, sat an enormous basket of gleaming fruit and tins of nuts. Such an expensive gift! Who would have sent it? She crouched down, sorting through the items. But what really caught her attention was a stack of sheet music. She released a soft cry as she carefully lifted the copy of "Stella by Starlight," featuring a woman in a blue dress framed by an enormous white moon behind her. The words, the notes, and the harmonies filled her mind. Soon she was humming the tune. And there was more music in the basket, Bing Crosby's "Swinging on a Star" included. A small envelope slipped free from where it had been tucked between the crisp sheets.

She opened it and slid out a pink card with music notes and flowers painted across the front.

Eileen,

I hope you don't mind. I took the liberty of ordering your music from Hampton's Music. May your days be filled with bright songs and laughter, for both you and your father. The best days are yet to come.

Your friend,

Rafe

# CHAPTER TWENTY-FIVE

I t was suppertime on Friday when Debbie reached Good Shepherd with another pastry box loaded with fresh goodies under her arm. A mourning dove cooed from a tree overhead, and she soaked in its music.

A bittersweet sound, yet so beautiful and haunting, reminding her of Reed. Time should have healed this wound, but there were aching moments when she thought of him and all she had lost. Her well-laid plans for her life had shattered in an instant with a single phone call.

The *clip-clop* of horses' hooves caught her off guard and pulled her out of her reverie. A black buggy rolled past the nursing home. Slowly.

As it passed, Debbie saw Benjamin Lapp's face. He didn't see her at first. He was staring toward the massive windows of the complex. But then his alarmed gaze collided with hers, and before she could say hello, he turned his face toward the street. With a snap of the reins and a cluck of his tongue, he urged the chestnut horses to a trot.

Her breathing quickened.

Why had he come to Good Shepherd? Was she overreacting to assume he was spying on Eileen? After all, Dennison had only so many streets. Inevitably, everyone would drive past the nursing home at some point.

She wasn't worried about the staff—the nurses and aides were professional in restricting visitors. But Eileen's generous nature might allow a visit, and Debbie wasn't certain Benjamin meant well.

Hadn't Annie's brother seen an Amish man driving away from the vandalized Buona Vita late at night?

When Debbie entered the small apartment, she found Eileen staring out the window.

"I thought I saw Samuel outside," the elderly woman muttered as she pulled back the lacy drapes. She gripped her walker with the other hand. "I was afraid I was imagining things at my age."

Anger threaded through Debbie as she set the box of pastries on the small kitchen table next to the living room. The open concept helped give an illusion of space, but just barely. From where she stood in the apartment, she had a good view of the road, thanks to the wide windows. Benjamin's slow drive-by seemed less and less benign.

"No, I saw the Amish man too. Benjamin Lapp, Samuel's great-nephew, rode past, though I have no idea why."

Using her walker, Eileen eased into the chair next to the window. Her gaze returned to the street. "Poor boy. His grandpa was so hard on his children. He worked them from sunup to sundown, and barely any rest. Nothing was more important to Jacob than his father's business."

"Benjamin's a troubled young man, to say the least," Debbie agreed as she handed Eileen a half-moon pie stuffed with tart cherries and wrapped in parchment paper.

"Maybe he's lonely." Eileen unwrapped the pie.

"My employee, Annie Butler, says her brother has seen an Amish man driving around town at night."

"Courting, perhaps?" Eileen suggested under her breath with a wistful expression.

"Or creating trouble. Ricky Carosi's restaurant was broken into, and so was the station."

*Oh dear.* She hadn't meant to share those tidbits with Eileen and worry her.

Eileen, however, didn't appear as concerned as Debbie felt. They sat in comfortable silence. Whimsical family photos lined the white walls. Rafe and Eileen next to the Eiffel Tower. The couple kissing at the Grand Canyon. Many of the photos included Kim, with pigtails and braces, clinging to one parent or the other. Later, Kim as a young woman. Perhaps the best photos were of the whole Palmer family together, beaming, their arms wrapped around each other. Despite the tiny apartment, Eileen seemed larger than life, sitting regally in a tufted chair.

"My dear girl—" After a nibble of the pie, Eileen sighed with delight. "Did you make this?"

"I wish. No one bakes quite like Janet. She says that by next week she'll have me making the pies."

"You're getting the hang of it. Your café breathes new life into the depot. I think it was really meant to be a place of joy and of folks coming together. Not saying goodbye, but staying awhile, visiting over coffee. A place to build community, and not to send folks so far into the world."

Debbie clasped her knees. "I couldn't have said it better myself. Dennison has always been a special place to me. It's good to be back among friends and family. I want the café to embody a sense of home."

"Maybe one day a young man will make Dennison even more home," Eileen said with a twinkle in her eye.

Debbie chuckled. Eileen probably got away with saying things most others wouldn't dare dream of uttering. And although she wasn't looking for a man to complete her life, she immediately pictured Greg.

Her phone rang, and she answered. She didn't recognize the number. Hopefully, it wasn't a telemarketer.

"I-is this Debbie Albright?" an unfamiliar male voice stammered after a moment of silence.

Debbie pressed the phone against her ear. "It is." Her heart took up a rapid beat.

A deep breath shuddered from the other side. "I got an email from Kim Smith, the museum director. She left her number and yours. I tried to call her first, but her voice mail is full and I couldn't leave a message, so I thought I'd try you."

"Is this Richard? Richard Brown?" Debbie struggled to keep from sounding breathless. At last. She had the elusive mystery man on the phone. Just as she and Kim had hoped, he had taken the bait and finally called.

"Are you going to eat your pie?" Eileen pointed to the uneaten pastry dripping with cherry filling and waiting on the small table next to Debbie's recliner. "Is that Kim on the phone? Tell Kim her mother wants to talk to her right now. I want to thank her for the music she sent the other day."

Debbie held her hand over the phone. "One moment, Eileen. No, it's not Kim, it's a man—"

"Uh—" The man paused. "Did you say Eileen?"

"Yes," Debbie answered. And immediately heard the beep of an ended call.

"Who is on the phone?" Eileen demanded as she adjusted her glasses.

"I'm not sure, but I think it was Richard Brown, the man who dropped off Samuel's letter." Debbie called the number back, but no one answered. She left a message, asking the man to return the call.

She had a sinking feeling she had lost Richard Brown for good.

The next morning, Debbie carried a tray of strawberry and vanilla whoopie pies to the bakery case. She slipped the tray onto the proper shelf while a group of school-aged kids stared at her from the nearest table. She could almost hear their stomachs growl with anticipation.

As she straightened, she dabbed her warm cheeks with the back of her hand. Sweltering humidity filled the station and the café during the late-morning rush. An exhausting morning.

First, she had informed Kim about the bizarre phone call with Richard. Kim had insisted on trying to call him herself. Debbie wasn't certain pushing Richard would help matters, but she also recognized that Kim would do exactly as Kim wished. Next, Greg had stopped by for a large cup of coffee. Conversation with him remained pleasant, but she couldn't shake the burden she'd been carrying all morning surrounding her latest visit with the Lapps and the fiasco that followed with Daniel's health. Or her frustration over Richard hanging up on her. He had sounded nervous, which also made her think of Benjamin stalking the nursing home and warning Debbie not to return to Lapp Lumber.

She could hardly blame Benjamin for his concern over his father's health. She certainly worried about Hannah, who appeared so lonely and in need of friendship. Did the Lapps push everyone away who got too close? Or was Benjamin hiding something foul, as Annie had hinted only a few days ago?

Someone tapped her shoulder, drawing her to the present.

"I need three whoopie pies for the table next to the door. Vanilla, please." Annie bustled around the counter, carrying an empty pot of coffee. She set the pot under the coffee maker as she nodded in the direction of the café's latest offering. Janet had insisted on trying new flavors to draw the crowd in. Her idea proved a marketing hit, with whoopie pies filled with cake batter and sprinkles, orange, lime, caramel, fudge, and more.

Debbie found a plate and grabbed the nearby tongs, carefully lifting the soft cookies loaded with creamy filling. She handed the plate to Annie.

"Kinda hot in here, isn't it?" Annie said.

"I'll check the thermostat." Debbie brushed her hair off her forehead.

Annie opened her mouth to say something, but another woman approached the counter with a scowl. "I've been waiting for tea for ten minutes. Is anyone going to help me?"

"Yes, ma'am. I'm so sorry for the delay," Annie answered contritely. "Your tea is coming next."

The woman tapped her fingernails against the glass, her frown deepening by the minute. Debbie offered her a complimentary cookie. Satisfied, the woman headed back to her table with a strawberry whoopie pie.

"Who orders hot tea in this weather?" Annie muttered under her breath. She sifted through the fragrant tea bags tucked inside a canister until she found the right flavor. "I'm sorry for complaining. I'll be okay. It's just been a busy, hot morning."

The thermostat was set at a reasonable level, but the air conditioner was working hard, and the temperature in the café was seventy-eight degrees. Far too hot for their customers' comfort.

Intent on finding a fan to help cool the dining area, Debbie left the café and entered the museum. The museum, which opened at ten, was a popular spot this morning. Visitors milled about the displays, fanning themselves with brochures while wiping sweat from their brows. "Boogie Woogie Bugle Boy" by the Andrews Sisters played over the speakers as Debbie searched for Kim. A quick peek into her office showed no sign of the museum director.

She rushed past the ticket booth with its brass grill separating customers from employees. One employee, a college student named Evan, raised his eyebrows when she approached the counter. "Any sign of Kim?" she asked him.

"I saw her outside, next to the museum cars."

The train cars perched on the lawn, including the lounge car with an old radio. The big-band music car contained plenty of tourists, but no Kim. That meant she was either at the newest travel car, under renovations for a future bed-and-breakfast experience, or the hospital car. The original Pullman bed-and-breakfast car had proven to be an enormous hit over the summer. The newest car sat at the edge of the grounds, closer to the parking lot.

Debbie ducked beneath the velvet ropes blocking off curious customers and pushed on the door. It opened easily, the blast of hot air more stifling than in the café. Above, the barrel ceiling and elaborate trim had been freshly painted in a muted white. The rich wood paneling appeared carefully cleaned and oiled. Had the workers left for lunch? A drop cloth covered part of one carpet in the tiny sitting room.

She edged sideways, avoiding the possibility of touching wet paint. Kim's desire for accreditation with the American Alliance of Museums meant that she preferred to oversee the renovations herself. She was a stickler for historical accuracy. Plenty of open doors throughout the depot meant she could duck in and out at a moment's notice and check the work.

Maybe Kim was responsible for the missing antiques, even if inadvertently.

Debbie's shoes were noiseless on the thick imitation Aubusson rug as she moved toward the bunk beds. "Kim, are you here?"

A door creaked at the end of the car, the sound chilling. Her breathing quickening, Debbie moved past an adorable miniature bathroom next to the bunk beds swathed in velvet curtains.

"Hello? Anyone there?"

The hot wind rippled the draped windows as she reached the end of the car. The exit door swung in the breeze before she grabbed the brass handle and poked her head outside. Had someone carelessly left the door open, neglecting to latch it properly?

She peered out of the car, turning her head left, then right. The brilliant sun momentarily blinded her. She squinted, shielded her face with one hand, and scanned the museum cars with milling visitors waiting for entrance. No one appeared suspicious or in a rush to escape the area. She'd have to ask Janet or Annie if anyone saw anything unusual. She closed the door and backtracked her steps, pausing when she passed another small bathroom to her left.

A ray of sunlight gleamed off something metal lying on the black-and-white tiled floor. Relief and confusion coursed through her as she squeezed into the narrow space and crouched to inspect the collection of dainty silver spoons and a series of framed photographs of soldiers climbing into the Pullman car bunks. Why had someone left these items here? What an odd place to store antiques. She looked behind the trash can and saw several gold-rimmed teacups, one tilted carelessly on its side.

A door opened and slammed from the end of the car.

"Who's in here?" a man demanded. "You're not supposed to be in the train cars under renovation. You get out right now!"

"It's just Debbie," she called. "No need to be alarmed."

Footsteps pounded down the hall, coming toward her. She groaned as she struggled to get to her feet in the tight bathroom.

Silas burst into view, his face reddened with effort and a vein bulging in his forehead.

"Debbie Albright! What are *you* doing in the museum cars?"

# CHAPTER TWENTY-SIX

Debbie sighed as she placed a hand against the wall to stabilize herself.

"I'm looking for Kim. The air-conditioning isn't working, and she's disappeared. One of the college staff said she was outside by the train cars." Debbie felt like a kid caught with her hand in her grandmother's cookie jar.

She felt her cheeks flame when Silas glared at her before dropping his gaze to the photos, teacups, and silver spoons. He panted for a few moments, his gray T-shirt damp around the neck and armpits like he had run across the hot pavement.

She pointed to the floor. "I found these antiques just lying here on the floor."

"I'm not surprised." Silas scowled. "I saw someone running across the grounds late last night. I was cleaning the main entrance doors when I saw the person. He bolted as soon as I ran out the door. Just now, I saw the door to this car ajar and figured the person had snuck inside."

"To hide the items and avoid being caught?" Debbie frowned.

Was someone taking things from the displays? Had they hastily abandoned their stash?

Silas winced. "So now the cars aren't locked at night. How did I miss this?"

He appeared so anguished Debbie wanted to comfort him.

"I'm gonna get fired." He ran a hand over his face. "After I saw that figure, I checked every inch of the station, but I didn't see anything else. Maybe I was so rattled I didn't lock up the way I should."

She didn't like the sound of a person running around the station late at night. Nor would Kim. Was Silas telling the truth?

Silas stepped back, allowing her to escape the claustrophobic space. "I thought I closed everything. I really did."

"Did you see the person's face last night?" Debbie asked.

"No." Silas sounded ragged. "Whoever it was, he wore a hooded sweatshirt, and the hood was pulled up so I couldn't see the face. Ran fast, though. Really fast."

A few minutes later, Debbie found Kim organizing the historical display that featured Eileen's years of service as the stationmaster. A life-sized black-and-white photo of her rested in the rectangular glass case. Next to the display, a mannequin shape wore Eileen's trim uniform of a fitted jacket and knee-length skirt. A pair of brown heels waited as if Eileen might step into them at any moment.

Below the case, a locked cabinet door housed more memorabilia, which Kim rotated regularly. Every so often, families of World War II veterans or employees of the train station donated items. Purple Heart medals, uniforms, doughnut recipes, train artifacts, and so much more. One woman mailed her grandfather's station sandwich bag, carefully preserved over the years as a canteen memento.

Kim carefully curated the pieces, donating some items to the National Veterans War Memorial and Museum in Columbus, Ohio. She kept what she could for Dennison, claiming that a fresh display every few months would encourage families to return and learn something new with each visit.

When Debbie told her what had happened and what she had found in the Pullman car, Kim was visibly upset. "I can't believe anyone would sneak around here late at night. I'm going to have to talk to Silas about checking doors. I'll check the security camera feed and call Ian."

Silas hadn't gone with Debbie to talk to Kim. His former bluster had disappeared, and he had looked ill, his bravado completely deflated as he parted ways with Debbie on her way to the station.

"Why was Silas at the train car this morning?" Kim demanded.

"I think he's trying to catch the thief. He says he saw someone running through the grounds last night."

Before Debbie could say more, someone cleared her throat.

Annie offered a cautious smile as she stepped into the room. "I'm so sorry to interrupt, but the café is getting pretty busy. I think we need some extra help."

"Let me know what you find, Kim," Debbie said before she followed Annie back to the café. Kim nodded, silent as she studied her mother's display.

How much of the conversation had Annie heard? She had often hovered close lately, working hard, by all appearances. Debbie mentally kicked herself for previously discussing Eileen's case with Janet so openly in the café. A lesson well-learned. She would need to be more discreet with her conversations in the future.

Annie rubbed her bare arms as if suddenly chilled. "You look troubled. Was something stolen again?"

"I'm looking into it. I found an assortment of Pullman items in one of the bathrooms."

Annie raised an eyebrow and held the café door open for Debbie to enter. "My dad said he feels nervous about me going to work on my own so early in the morning."

Debbie forced a smile onto her face. "Dennison is one of the safest places you'll ever find."

"Good. I'd hate to think of anyone hurting the museum. My brother said he keeps seeing a young Amish man late at night, riding around town. You never know who you can trust."

Debbie didn't respond, but her mind easily conjured an image of Benjamin dumping papers into a burning barrel and driving past Good Shepherd. She'd love to understand why Hannah and her brother remained at odds over the papers. She hated to think a young man would stoop so low as to stalk Eileen and possibly frighten her.

Yet something didn't feel quite right about Annie's gossip. "By the way, as much as I love having you work for the café, do you need to register for school? Aren't the dates for registering this week?"

Annie waved a hand, but her eye contact wavered. "I'm going to be just fine. Besides, I didn't want to leave you in a pinch without the right person to replace me."

"I appreciate your willingness to work," Debbie answered slowly. "But you don't need to stay because of any obligation on our part. No one wants to miss the first week of classes for any reason, not even a summer job. You can't make up lost sessions so easily. Besides,

Janet and I will find other workers. Paulette Connor will be back September first."

"Of course. I really appreciate the job and the opportunity to save extra cash," Annie said as she moved toward the register. "I'll certainly miss this place when I leave. Can I get back to you on the end date?"

"Sure." Debbie nodded. If Annie had arranged for a later date, then that was between her and the university.

Annie smoothed her braid. "You know, I've been thinking a lot about the Unnamed Soldier you and Kim discussed the other day. If someone discovered his name, they could get like a reward or something, right? Imagine what a historical society would do for information like that. It must be worth something good."

"I think the value is more sentimental and historical than anything," Debbie replied. "I can't say what a museum would offer for such information, but it wouldn't be oodles of cash."

Annie shrugged. "I suppose you're right. But I wonder if Richard knew something about that letter that we don't know."

"I'm not sure what he knows, and I no longer have the letter," Debbie said. Why was Annie so interested?

"Who has it?" Annie pressed.

"The Lapp family," Debbie answered after a pause. "Eileen wanted them to read it. We don't know for sure how many letters they received from Samuel. It might be nice to have one final keepsake."

Annie's look of shock made Debbie regret sharing.

The young woman shook her head. "I hope that boy, Benjamin, has nothing to do with the museum's troubles. I sure didn't feel comfortable around him. Did you see the way he stared at me when he came in here the other day?"

Debbie bit the inside of her cheek. She hadn't noticed anything quite like what Annie described. Had she missed something going on between Annie and Benjamin?

After finding Kim again and reporting the problem with the air-conditioning, Debbie forced herself to focus on the tasks at hand, including filling an order for an elderly couple. As she settled their sandwiches on a plate for Annie to serve, she mulled over the strange morning.

Only a few tables had customers, and no one appeared in a hurry. The tourist crowd today had fewer children and teenagers and more elderly guests. In fact, Annie was serving only two tables. Why had Annie insisted Debbie return to help with a rush that wasn't happening?

# CHAPTER TWENTY-SEVEN

*Dennison McCluskey Park's flower gardens bloomed, each bed spilling over with petunias. Newly painted lampposts and benches spruced up the green lawn. For the past few years, Eileen had skirted the park. She tended to avoid her former meeting place with Samuel as much as possible. But today, she found herself actually eager to meet Rafe beneath the rustling trees. He'd promised to bring lunch, courtesy of Alberto's kitchen. Surely she would find cannoli or something wonderful in the picnic basket.*

*The sun beamed brightly overhead. Papa rested at home, thanks to the intervention of a widowed neighbor, who had kindly offered to sit and read in the living room just in case he woke from a nap and wandered.*

Eileen inhaled a deep breath and released it, feeling the tension escape right down to her toes. A thrum of excitement filled her when she glanced at the bench where new sheet music lay. She couldn't wait to surprise Rafe with the latest songs. His voice far surpassed hers any day.

"Eileen!" She whirled around when her name was called, and to her delight, Rafe walked toward her with a large basket hooked over his arm.

She stood, placing her fists on her hips. "You're late, Mr. Palmer, and I'm positively famished. I thought I could smell Buona Vita's pasta from here."

He laughed and raised the basket in triumph. "It'll be worth the wait, I promise. Alberto made something special just for you."

After he sank onto the bench, he flipped the basket lid open, offering her a glimpse into the red checkered interior.

"My, my," she breathed. "Alberto made us tiramisu."

A bowl of espresso-soaked ladyfinger cookies layered with rich cream, mascarpone, and cocoa beckoned from within the basket.

Rafe grinned. "I told you it would be worth the wait."

She scanned the garlic knots, a casserole dish with pasta, and the largest and likely spiciest meatballs she had ever seen. Her mouth watered.

Rafe pulled out two small ceramic plates and a pair of cloth napkins. As he handed her a spoon and a fork, another sound shattered the quiet of the park. The clip-clop of a horse and the creak of a buggy easing to a stop forced her to raise her head.

Dread filled her the moment she recognized Jacob.

With the bench situated close to the road, she had no choice but to look into his fierce blue eyes, blazing with unconcealed rage.

"Well, if it is not Jezebel herself. Forgot my bruder so soon, did you?"

She could only stare, her chest numb and cold inside as Jacob turned to Rafe, his lip curled in scorn. Rafe slowly rose, casting an elongated shadow across the sidewalk.

Jacob pointed at Eileen. "She is trouble. If you know what is good for you, you will leave her alone."

Rafe waited a beat before responding, his voice soft but firm. "There's no call for such rudeness. If you can't be polite, then I think it's you who should leave."

Jacob snorted as he grasped the reins with a white-knuckled grip. "You do not know Eileen Turner like I do. She betrayed my bruder after talking him into enlisting in the war. Look how easily she replaced the so-called love of her life." His bright, hard gaze slid to the papers scattered on the bench, a gift intended for Rafe. "She had the nerve to buy Samuel books. Get out while you still can."

Rafe didn't move. "We don't want any trouble. Good day, sir."

Eileen rose, joining Rafe. "Jacob, you know I'm sorry about Samuel. I've tried to explain myself over and over. It was you who told me Samuel would never return home and to forget him. Please believe me when I said I never intended to hurt you or your family."

"Ja? It is too late for regrets. What is the name of your new liebling?"

She refused to expose Rafe, but he merely squared his shoulders.

"Rafe Palmer. I'm Alberto Carosi's nephew. I'm sorry for the loss of your brother, but we are grateful for his service to his country. Your family can be proud of him."

Jacob leaned forward, still gripping the reins while the horse pawed at the ground. "Do not presume to understand our ways, Englischer." He snapped the reins, and the buggy jerked forward, leaving Eileen alone again with Rafe.

She covered her mouth. When she regained her composure, she dropped her hand. "I can explain, Rafe. I—"

He held up a hand, pausing her midspeech. "I know about Samuel, Eileen. Harry told me when I painted the train station. I know Samuel willingly enlisted and he never came back to Dennison."

"I fear it's all my fault. The Amish are pacifists. They don't believe in hurting anyone, but this family is sure I hurt them terribly. How can I ever forgive myself for the damage I've unwittingly done? I'm certain they will never forgive me."

"No, they may never forgive you. Only God moves a heart to do so. But I wouldn't carry this weight forever. Samuel was old enough to decide his future, and he signed the enlistment papers all by himself. I met men from every background you can imagine during my time in the service. Rich and poor, from the city and the country—we all believed in our cause. We fought because we loved our families back home and saw no choice but to defend them." He touched her cheek. "Samuel made his choices, and there's no shame in loving him."

She glanced at Rafe, overwhelmed by the compassion she saw.

His Adam's apple bobbed. "But I must ask, do you still love Samuel?"

*The question sank deep within her, startling in the implications sure to follow. Was there room in her heart for Rafe? To love him as he so clearly desired? Could she allow herself to completely trust again? She wasn't quite certain what to say, and in her hesitation, Rafe's expression shuttered. He lowered his hand from her cheek and returned to the bench alone.*

# CHAPTER TWENTY-EIGHT

*L*ater that same Saturday, Debbie met with Janet, Ian, and Kim in Kim's office. Everyone stared at Kim's computer where a black-and-white security video played on the screen. Debbie studied the grainy footage, a little discombobulated. Following the hectic morning of discovering the hidden antiques, the rest of the day had felt off-kilter.

Just as Silas noted, someone had crept to the train station late last night. Silas startled before moving to the entrance, a cloth in hand to clean the glass door. He looked around wildly, nearly dropping the bucket in his haste, while the figure in black bolted. Rushing outside, Silas looked up and down the sidewalk.

"I think Silas might have prevented a second break-in. He surprised whoever came to the museum," Ian said as he stared at the screen.

"They certainly surprised him," Kim said. "I think he's on the waiting list for new hearing aids from the VA hospital. He was definitely caught off guard. I'm relieved he didn't get hurt."

"I wonder if someone knew about his hearing loss and snuck in before, taking advantage of the open door and his inability to hear well," Debbie said. "It wouldn't be hard to sneak past him, if you were careful." She suppressed a shudder at the image of the ominous figure.

"They might not even have had to break in," Kim said, shaking her head. She drew in a deep breath then let it out slowly. "I've left my office open plenty of times, lulled by a sense of safety. Silas and I have worked long hours over the summer, both of us in the building at the same time and assuming the other took care to lock up. We're both responsible, and we need to communicate better with each other as to who locks up and when. Although he's so shaken up after this last event, he might just move in with his daughter and finally retire. Let's play the video again."

The video at least proved that Silas hadn't stolen the kitchen antiques. Relieved for him, Debbie felt some of her tension lift. Hopefully, Kim and Silas could agree on how to best proceed in the days to come.

Kim froze an image on the monitor. A lean figure in a black hooded sweatshirt and carrying a duffel bag disappeared into the night.

"Interesting. Did this person plan to steal more goods and nearly got caught, so he left them in the Pullman car? I wonder what the next target might be." Ian tapped his chin. "Care to look over the grounds with me, Kim?"

Debbie wanted more than anything to search the grounds with Ian and Kim, but the café demanded her full attention. Ian dropped by the café later, his police uniform and aviator sunglasses drawing plenty of attention from customers. With a flirtatious grin directed at Janet, he snagged a slice of apple kuchen—Hannah's heirloom recipe. Of all the recipes, this had proved the final winner.

He nodded when Janet offered him a steaming cup of coffee to go with the kuchen.

Debbie joined him and Janet at a booth.

Ian stirred cream into his coffee. "I've chatted with Silas. Unfortunately, he's searched high and low for the remaining items and found nothing. No one seems to know a thing."

Debbie remembered Ricky's break-in as well. A troubling thought clouded her mind.

"Could someone have a vendetta against Eileen's family? Kim is Eileen's daughter and runs the museum. Ricky is family, connected to Eileen's husband, Rafe Palmer. And…" Debbie paused, uncertain how to express herself without hurting Hannah Lapp. She took a deep breath. "Becky, the wife of our electrician, is Eileen's niece. She's had issues with the Lapp family. Daniel Lapp won't honor an order Becky made. He claims to have no record of it. What if everything is linked somehow? Annie said her brother saw a young Amish man driving his buggy out of Buona Vita's parking lot late one night. I saw Benjamin Lapp driving by Good Shepherd the other day. Could these events be related? Could someone be specifically targeting Eileen and her family?"

A shiver rippled through her as soon as she admitted the nagging idea that kept her up at night.

Ian's eyebrows shot up. "Is Annie available for a chat?" His Scottish brogue deepened. "It sounds like I need to visit Benjamin Lapp as well."

"I'll get her for you," Debbie offered.

She frowned as she checked the kitchen. No Annie. A figure moved outside the window, gesturing wildly with one arm while speaking on the phone. Her cheeks flushed, Annie's rage was palpable. The conversation must have cut off, because she shoved the phone into her pocket.

Debbie opened the door just as Annie pivoted on her heel. She stared at Debbie, her eyes round as saucers. Then she blinked and offered a bright smile.

"Is anything wrong, Annie?"

Annie shook her head. "No, everything's fine."

Debbie held the door open. "Chief Shaw is questioning the staff regarding the missing antiques and display case. You got a minute to chat with him?"

Annie fingered her braid as she entered the kitchen. "I—I guess. Should I go right now? I hate to leave Janet alone at the counter."

"I think you should go right away," Debbie advised. "I'm certain Chief Shaw won't take long. He just spoke with Kim and most of the other staff. He's in the dining room. I'll help Janet with the customers in the meantime."

Annie fidgeted with the apron strings at her waist. "I should let you know I found a roommate. My last day of work may be soon. I can give you a few more days, but that's probably it."

"Sure," Debbie said. "That shouldn't be a problem, although I might need to mail the check to you. Can you leave your new address?"

"Uh—yeah, I guess I can leave an address for you," Annie said as she walked toward the museum.

Debbie frowned at the odd response, but before she could say anything, her phone rang.

# CHAPTER TWENTY-NINE

*Dennison, Ohio*
*September 1946*

*The medicinal smells mingled with tangy sarsaparilla and other sweets tickled Eileen's nose. The Revco drugstore no longer beckoned to her the way it had when she was a high school student.*

*She waited for Papa's most recent prescription to be filled. Through the years, the interior of the drugstore had remained the same, the tall glass jars stacked with peppermint sticks and other penny candy. Behind the soda counter, a long gilt mirror reflected her image. She stopped by the swivel stools that lined the counter, surprised at the spark of joy she saw in her reflection. Months ago, she had called Rafe on the phone, surprising him, considering how she had left things unsaid at the picnic. When she had boldly asked him on a date to a local concert—him driving, of course—he had laughed with delight. Since then, they had been together, enduring the teasing of friends. She wanted to take things slow and, thankfully, Rafe understood.*

*The other day, Papa had given her a big hug and said, "My dear girl, I've never seen you so happy. It does my heart a world of good to hear you sing again."*

*She chuckled at the thought of her sweet papa always ready to welcome Rafe with open arms. Perhaps hearing her laughter, the pharmacist rustled in from the back room. "Good afternoon, Miss Turner. I'll have the order to you in just a minute."*

*"I'm not in a hurry," she called out as she stood by the soda fountain.*

*A man moved at the end of the drugstore, next to the aisle of creams and glass bottles, his face pinched as he held a white tin of medicated ointment, Thomas Leeming & Co.'s Ben-Gay.*

*She gripped the counter to keep from stumbling. "Samuel? Is that you?"*

*When he raised his head at the sound of her voice, she realized her mistake.*

*"No, Jezebel. It is Jacob." He intentionally bumped her shoulder as he sauntered past then plunked a handful of coins next to the cash register to pay for the ointment.*

*"It's Miss Turner to you."*

A muscle jumped in the hollow of Jacob's jaw. "Ja, but for how long? I have watched you with that Palmer man these past months." He moved toward her, blocking her escape. "Would you sing with me, I wonder?" He reached out a hand to grab her arm, and she slapped it away.

"Don't you dare touch me! You are not Samuel's replacement."

His eyes darkened, molten with hatred and something else she didn't fully understand. "Neither is Palmer. But like I said, I have seen you two in the park."

Ice spread through her veins. Had Jacob been spying on her and Rafe? She had nothing to hide. Once a week, they ate at Buona Vita or they took a walk through McCluskey Park. Lately, she had taken to inviting Rafe to have dinner with her and Papa at her house. In every situation, Rafe had proven to be a perfect gentleman, considerate and kind.

Anger swiftly replaced her fear. "My life is none of your concern."

"I would hate to see another man ruined because of you. I have heard that the depot will hire someone far more appropriate and mature for stationmaster."

"What do you mean?"

He inched closer. "Someone sent a few anonymous tips."

*Dismay sent a nauseating flash of heat through her, chasing the ice. No wonder her boss had sounded so concerned over the telephone. Yet he had defended her all the same, finally praising her efforts and dedication. She would remain stationmaster for as long as she could. But would the townspeople believe Jacob's false insinuations? Surely most of them would realize she loved her job and did her best to serve the town. "You have no right to slander my name."*

*A grim smile curved his lips as he pushed on the door to leave the drugstore. "I have every right to speak the truth. I want everyone to know who you really are."*

*Her frustration burst out of her before she could summon the strength to remain silent. "Samuel would be so disappointed in your behavior. His faith made him the compassionate man that he was. What you've done is* not *the way of the Ordnung. So which one of you is the brother who is holding to his Amish values?"*

*"You never knew my bruder, even though you fancy you did." As the door slammed in his wake, Jacob's parting words brought a stab of shock. "Thank Gott Samuel never saddled himself with you. I made certain of it."*

# CHAPTER THIRTY

With one hour until closing time on Saturday, Debbie's phone dinged, following perhaps the wildest workday in the café's short history, with missing items, Kim's disturbing video feed, and Annie's strange behavior. She picked up the phone, her voice breathless with anticipation. "Hello?"

"Hi Debbie, it's Cheryl, from the Swiss Miss. Is this a good time to chat?"

Debbie glanced around. Janet was filling a pastry box with cherry whoopie pies, while Harry entered the café, leaning on his cane. Behind him came his granddaughter, Patricia, who often came to the café for peppermint mocha coffee. Becky also followed, an infant carrier on her arm.

"Well, we're in the middle of a late afternoon rush, but I can call you once we close. Good news, I hope?" Annie hadn't returned yet from her visit with Ian, leaving Debbie short-staffed yet again.

"I think you'll be very interested in what I have to share with you. I got ahold of Frank Raber's daughter, Linda. She rummaged through her dad's letters, and yes, he corresponded with Samuel Lapp during and after the war. They met in the Pacific and formed a tight bond, since both of them came from Amish homes. It's quite a story, when you have time."

"Give me an hour, maybe less, and I'll be free to chat," Debbie promised. A thrill rippled through her at the idea of discovering something tangible about Samuel.

"I can tell by your face you received good news," Janet said under her breath as she grabbed the coffeepot. "I think we could all use good news this afternoon, especially considering what we saw on that security feed."

"Cheryl from the Swiss Miss finally heard from Frank Raber's daughter. It turns out he knew Samuel Lapp. Linda saved their correspondence."

Janet whistled. "Not too many ex-Amish men in the military, that's for sure. How incredible that they found each other!"

Debbie had to agree. She waved at Harry, pleased to see him healthy enough to return to the café. He slowly eased into a booth with his granddaughter's help, and Janet stopped by the table to take his order. If Debbie had to guess, it would include mochas and muffins.

Muffins which sorely needed restocking. She headed for the kitchen, intending to find more chocolate chip and blueberry muffins. As she reached for the nearest tray stored on a bakery trolley, her momentary triumph was short-lived. She couldn't help but wonder how the Lapps and Eileen might receive the news that Samuel had survived the war. One undeniable fact rose to the surface, a fact with the power to hurt.

Samuel Lapp had chosen not to return home.

Harry and Patricia didn't linger long at the café. Crosby waited patiently, his tail wagging. Patricia slid an extra dollar bill into the tip jar next to the register. "Thank you for watching out for my grandfather when he comes in. He so enjoys it here. It's his favorite part of the day."

Debbie found a set of tongs near the treat display and placed an extra pair of cookies in a bag for Harry to take home. "We've missed him. I'm glad he's feeling better. He tells the most wonderful stories to any customer willing to listen. It's our joy to fill him up with treats and coffee."

Debbie waved goodbye to Harry and Patricia before serving Becky. It was moments like these, the pleasure of connecting with and serving others, that kept her heart fueled. No matter the stress of running the café, she really needed to savor such blissful moments. Harry's delight in returning to the station brought a lightness to Debbie's step as she stopped at Becky's booth.

"Want to join me for coffee? Decaf, if you have it." Becky slid over in the booth to make space. Her daughter slept soundly in an infant carrier despite the noise. Debbie cooed over the precious girl, who resembled a Gerber baby with perfect lips. Nestled in a pale green and pink cotton blanket, the baby rested her plump cheek against a dimpled fist.

After grabbing two cups of coffee, decaf as requested, Debbie joined her friend. "I've got a moment or two to chat with you. I'm so glad you came to visit. Abby is adorable. Every time I see her I can't believe how big she's gotten."

Becky smiled. "Naps are improving. I finally got a few hours of sleep while Mark took care of her the other day. It's amazing what a lack of sleep can do to a person. The clouds are clearing from my mind."

"I'm glad you're getting rest. Did you get your furniture order resolved with Daniel Lapp?" Debbie paused before sipping her coffee.

Becky's eyes filled with tears. She brushed one aside with her thumb. "We met with him earlier today. His daughter, Hannah, is amazing. She searched through all the orders her father wrote over the past three months. Unfortunately, the paperwork she found doesn't include the second set of bedroom furniture. I feel so bad, Debbie. I looked and looked through my own paperwork, and I couldn't find the Lapp receipt. I must have thrown it away with a takeout bag or some other garbage. Would you believe Mark and I combed through our trash bags in the dumpster, searching for that yellow slip? I wrongly assumed Daniel had messed up the order and overquoted the price. He didn't. I made the error. Hannah showed me her slip, and I felt terrible and apologized to her and the family. I had to do the right thing and call my customer and explain the entire situation. I took the fall. My customer really wants the furniture and will wait for Daniel to finish the additional pieces. I've offered to discount my original fee. It's been a humbling lesson, for sure. I'm so embarrassed. I shouldn't have been so quick to blame the Lapp family."

Debbie felt compassion, not to mention conviction, for her initial judgment regarding the senior Lapp. "I'm so glad the situation is resolved."

Becky drew a shaky breath as she tucked the blanket around her sleeping daughter. "Me too. When I dropped by Lapp Lumber this morning, I heard about Daniel's trip to the hospital. Part of me feared I had done something to him or somehow added to his stress."

"Is he feeling better?" Debbie asked as she cradled the warm cup. Her hands felt suddenly cold and clammy. *Lord, keep Daniel safe. Forgive me for my false assumptions regarding this situation.*

"Hannah is forcing her father to rest at home. His son, Benjamin, seemed rattled by the event. But both men assured me the furniture will arrive, albeit a few weeks late. I can live with a small delay. I hope Daniel continues to rest as much as he needs."

"I hope both you and Daniel will get the rest you need. I hope your business will prosper and you'll get your dream home soon."

Becky raised her cup in a toast before draining it. "Me too, Debbie. Thanks for the coffee and the chat."

Just as Becky left the café with her sleeping baby, Annie entered with Ian, her expression subdued as she filled a bucket with water and washed the tables next to the windows. Ian greeted Janet with a kiss on the cheek.

"Any leftover kuchen in that kitchen of yours?" he asked in a hopeful voice that made Debbie grin. "I'd take a second slice home, if I could."

Janet patted his cheek. "I'll see if I can bake something tomorrow for you. Honestly, Debbie and I have been running nonstop, trying to figure out what's happening with Samuel Lapp and Richard Brown."

Ian pursued his lips. "Maybe you can send me with another cup of coffee?"

Debbie found a paper cup and filled it with steaming coffee while nervous expectancy warred with her impatience. Closing time was just around the corner, and she wanted nothing more than to have the answers she craved. After placing a lid on the cup, she offered it to Ian, who held a bag of treats, thanks to Janet.

When Annie went into the kitchen with a pail of soapy water, Debbie lowered her voice. "I just heard from Cheryl at the Swiss Miss. She has a friend, Linda, whose father, Frank Raber, became friends with Samuel Lapp during World War II. I was about to call her, and then I think we ought to go to Lapp Lumber. We might have some solid information to offer Hannah about her long-lost great-uncle."

"I'll be ready in a jiff," Janet said. She propped her fists on her hips. "I'm not missing this meeting. I'm going with you."

Ian smiled as he headed toward the exit.

Debbie flipped the sign on the door to closed while Janet emptied the register, placing the cash in a vinyl bag to deposit at the bank on their way. Annie brought a fresh bucket of water and finished washing the tables, her movements just as swift as Debbie's. In fact, the young woman appeared in a hurry.

"I've got to run in a few minutes. Is there anything else you need me to do for closing?" she asked.

"No, we've got it. I had the kitchen mostly cleaned before Ian showed up," Janet answered. "Debbie and I will lock up. You're free to go."

Annie paused as she untied her apron. "If you have to leave, I can close. It's no trouble at all."

Debbie felt a gut check. Over the past month, she had been content to let Annie enjoy increasing responsibility at the café, and as a result, the museum. She strove to keep her voice level, reminding herself of the security cameras recently installed in the museum sections, thanks to Mark and Greg. "No, that's okay. We're done for the day. Have a good night, Annie. We'll see you Monday morning, bright and early."

Annie hung her apron on the hook without another word, although she offered a slight smile. She retrieved her purse and shut the door behind her. No one waited for her in the parking lot. Instead, she climbed into the driver's seat of the same rusted yellow Corvette her brother drove.

Janet fished her keys out of her purse. "Let's call Cheryl and get some answers."

# CHAPTER THIRTY-ONE

**D**ebbie watched as Janet, wife of the police chief of Dennison, did everything possible not to speed in traffic.

"We're hitting every single red light," her friend whined under her breath as she gripped the steering wheel.

"You're pretty anxious to get there," Debbie said with a chuckle.

"I guess I am." Janet grinned. "But I thought you weren't welcome at Lapp Lumber anymore?"

Debbie grinned back. "I figure the worst they can do is tell me to leave." She shrugged. "Besides, I have information I hope Hannah will be glad to get. I'm not going to make her miss out on that because her father and brother are unreasonable."

The red light turned green, and Janet stepped on the gas, lurching her car forward just as Debbie called Cheryl.

Thankfully, Cheryl answered. "Hello?" Static made the reception flicker in and out.

"Hi Cheryl, this is Debbie, returning your call."

"I'm putting you on speakerphone so Naomi can hear you. She's at my house, making the most wonderful chicken and dumplings for supper. Wish you could join us."

"Janet and I would love to have supper with you—maybe in a few weeks, once our schedule slows down? We're on our way to Lapp

Lumber right now. Hannah wants to know more about her great-uncle. I can't speak for the Lapp men, but please, share what you found. I'll put the phone on speaker too, so Janet can listen."

Debbie refrained from burdening Cheryl with Benjamin's strange behavior. She raised the phone's volume to its maximum setting.

Cheryl's voice came through loud and clear. "Of course. I promised you a story. I already told you that our church has a cottage we reserve for women who are escaping abusive situations. A few years ago, when we were first renovating the building, a friend of mine tore down some of the rotting walls and discovered a few mason jars loaded with vintage coins stacked between the walls. Inside the jars were also letters written from a soldier who sounded remarkably Amish. We discovered his name was Frank Raber.

"Determined only to heal and not kill, Frank worked as a medic in the Pacific. When he returned home, he married. But he couldn't go back to his family, even though he wanted to reconcile. They wanted nothing to do with him, although, obviously, someone kept his letters and hid them in the walls. We were able to trace the letters to him, but he had passed away. His daughter, Linda, was thrilled to get the letters, as you can imagine."

Debbie held her breath as she listened. Janet kept her gaze on the road.

Cheryl continued after a deep breath. "Here's where it gets really good." Her voice quivered with excitement. "Frank saved a man's life at Iwo Jima, when the marines took back the mountain from the Japanese. Frank corresponded with an Amish man—get ready for it—named Samuel, who fought with the marines. I'm going to read you one of Linda's letters."

"Oh, wow," Janet whispered. She slowed the car and pulled over to the curb. This time, she didn't complain about the stop.

"Are you there?" Cheryl asked.

"We're listening," Debbie responded. Her heart pounded as she held the phone.

Cheryl cleared her throat and began to read.

"'Dear Frank, when you hid me in the foxhole, I thought for sure I would die. I had bounced over rugged terrain and volcanic sand, slung over the shoulder of a fellow marine—one who refused to give up, even when bullets zinged past us, left and right. At first, I did not believe Gott heard my prayers for safety. I was wrong. Gott surrounded all of us with His infinite love and care during the darkest of nights.

"'The 5th Marine Division, *Semper Fi,* proved their mettle during a banzai charge from the Japanese at dusk. A horrible realization hit me as soon as you struggled to bandage my leg with only twilight to guide your hands while another savior traded fire, drawing the enemy away from you and me hiding in that awful hollow tucked behind the brush and rock. I was not born to fight, Frank. You know how hard it is for an Amish man to pick up a weapon and charge another human being made in the image of Gott. Yes, you know this truth more than most. How naive I was to think I could make a difference in this broken world of ours. Not even military training could change my inner being.

"'Gott spared me that night, weak and trembling as I was. I was terrified when the order came to take the mountain. Surrounded by craggy hills and sand full of sharp, jagged rocks leading to the top of a dormant volcano, I felt as though I had traveled to another world. No longer was I on Amish farmland, with friends and safe neighbors on every side. Danger lay in the underground bunkers and pillboxes. When the shells thudded into the dirt several feet from where I stood, I froze. Something hit me, and I fell to the ground. I never saw the face of the man who rescued me. I heard his voice yelling above the din, ordering me to hang on and live.'"

Papers rustled across the connection. Cheryl spoke again.

"'In the months following my convalescence in a field hospital, I had time to ponder many things. I am so grateful I found you, a kindred friend, who understands the Amish ways and the desire tearing me from within, a desire to do so much more with my life. I thought fighting was the answer. I was wrong. I am finally at peace with who I am. I cannot change the world with a sword, but I can shape it with a pen. I am forever your devoted friend, Samuel.'"

Cheryl stopped reading, and the phone crackled over the speaker. Naomi's sweet voice cut in. "There are several other letters signed by Samuel. He swore Frank to secrecy, to never tell another soul about his journalism for the newspapers. I understand Samuel later helped change the conditions of the field hospitals. He challenged the prisoner-of-war treatment. He worried over the displaced children he encountered, especially the orphans. He helped raise money for orphanages."

"The Unnamed Soldier," Debbie said with a sense of awe as Janet put the vehicle in gear and rejoined traffic. "We've read some of his writing for the papers. Richard Brown, who left Samuel's letter for Eileen, also searched for the same articles. Why didn't Samuel reveal his actual name if he wrote for the *New York Times* and other big papers?"

"Sharing his true name could be viewed as pride." Naomi hesitated. "It is difficult to completely abandon one's way of life and beliefs. The Amish do not seek accolades or fame. Samuel, however, rose to the top. Maybe he felt freer to speak the truth from behind a veil of anonymity. His letters show a great desire to be alone. I should also add that he was injured in battle. Shrapnel to his left leg kept him from moving around much."

"So he's the missing journalist who nearly won a Pulitzer for his description of the war conditions," Janet mused as she drove.

"Ja, Samuel was a humble man, at the very least. I do not think he cared whether he won an award. He just wanted to be free to create," Naomi said.

"Do we know who carried Samuel through enemy lines?" Debbie asked.

Naomi spoke first. "To answer your question, Cheryl and I have wrestled with the information. Only Frank's name is mentioned during the Battle of Iwo Jima."

"Do you know where Samuel lived after the war?" Debbie gripped her armrest.

Papers rustled from the other side of the phone before Cheryl answered. "Hard to say. The men never met in person again, although they wrote and called each other over the years. But California was mentioned in one letter. Does that help?"

Excitement shot through Debbie as she recalled the letter in the burning barrel at Lapp Lumber. Richard's return address had been in California.

Janet made the final turn before they'd reach the lumberyard. "We have to tell the Lapp family. I hope they receive the news well."

Another pause, this time weighty. Naomi answered again, her voice filled with warning. "You should know that Samuel mentioned his bruder, Jacob, in several of the letters. Jacob warned Samuel to never return home. He told him no one wanted him, not even friends or loved ones. Jacob claimed the family and community had shunned Samuel and never wanted to see his face again, and if he returned home, judgment would come."

# CHAPTER THIRTY-TWO

**D**ebbie remained silent in the car as they pulled into Lapp Lumber, her mind reeling from what Naomi had shared over the phone. How could Jacob be so cruel as to discourage Samuel from returning home? Why the horrible lies?

She sat up straight when she saw Ian's black-and-white police car with large lettering reading DENNISON POLICE parked in front of the furniture store. Golden evening sunlight bronzed the buildings and grounds with a warm glow—a peaceful setting, but Debbie dreaded the encounter waiting inside the lumberyard. Regardless, she knew she had to share the truth with Hannah and learn what she could for Eileen's sake.

Janet chuckled. "That sneaky husband of mine. He didn't say a word about coming here."

Debbie reached for the door handle. "I, for one, am very glad he's here."

"Jacob despised his brother," Janet murmured as she turned off the car. "How can we be sure his hatred didn't pass to his son and grandson?"

"We can't be certain of anything," Debbie replied slowly. "But we can pray for wisdom. And we can pray for a family to experience healing after so many years of misunderstanding and betrayal."

*Lord, help us be instruments of peace to this family, especially Hannah and Eileen. Soften Daniel's and Benjamin's hearts.*

Debbie finished her silent prayer as she strode to the entrance. A strange sight greeted her inside the store. Ian had his hand on Benjamin's shoulder, comforting the young man. A tall police officer decked out in full uniform soothing a teary-eyed Amish man wasn't a sight Debbie figured she would see often.

"I'm so sorry, so very sorry," Benjamin muttered. "I knew it was wrong to lie—"

Daniel and Hannah stood next to Benjamin, listening intently to his halting speech. Hannah gasped when she saw Debbie and Janet, and everyone stopped to stare.

"I must apologize for interrupting." Debbie held up a hand. "I realize you don't want me here, but if you give me a moment, I think you'll find it worth your time."

When no one protested, she continued, her voice shaking. "I just got off the phone with Cheryl Miller from Sugarcreek. She helped us discover some interesting things about Samuel. We felt you should know what he did during the war. Yes, he fought as a marine at Iwo Jima and survived. However, there is enough evidence to suggest that he wrote for several prestigious newspapers under a pseudonym, bringing needed attention to the conditions of the field hospitals. He helped improve the medical care men received. He drew attention to the plight of hurting children overseas. In many ways, his writing pleaded for compassion and more aid to assist the orphans. He was an advocate for peace."

Dare she admit that Jacob discouraged Samuel from returning home? Caution held her back for the moment.

Daniel raised his eyebrows, and for a moment Debbie feared he might have trouble breathing a second time. But he appeared almost relieved. "My oncle wrote about needy children," he repeated softly. "I had always been told he had completely abandoned his faith."

Debbie shook her head. "No, not at all."

"I am so grateful you've told us." Hannah gestured for Debbie and Janet to come closer. "My bruder has also shared some import-ant things with the police chief."

Without his hat, Benjamin appeared even younger and more vulnerable. "Ja, I have some things to confess."

He sniffed loudly before taking the handkerchief Hannah extended to him. "I must apologize for my rudeness to you ladies. And to you, Hannah. Daed and I received a letter from California a few months back, and when we opened it, we discovered a man named Richard Brown claiming to be Samuel's son. Not only did he want to meet the family, but he wanted to tell us more about Samuel. Daed was cautious, but curious. Our dawdi hated Samuel. He shared awful stories about his lost bruder. Dawdi warned us that Samuel owned half of Lapp Lumber. If there was no Samuel, then the entire business belonged to Daed and me. I was so fright-ened we would lose the business to Richard. Dawdi always swore Samuel proved himself a selfish man who had never worked a day in his life. Worse, he nearly killed his maam, by running away to the war. But from what you've just shared, maybe Dawdi didn't tell us the entire story."

A jolt shot through Debbie as she eyed Janet. Richard Brown was Samuel's son!

After a pause, Daniel spoke to his children. "I do not think Dawdi understood the truth about his bruder. Lately I have wondered if he grossly exaggerated those old tales."

Benjamin cast a grief-stricken gaze at his sister. "I burned Richard's letters and Dawdi's collection of Samuel's letters in the barrel, just as you suspected. Richard wanted to meet at our home, and at first Daed agreed. Then Daed wondered if the train station might be better. Why not meet on neutral ground? But I did not want to meet Richard at all. I did not want him to see what he could claim as his inheritance. Daed and I have worked hard to make Lapp Lumber what it is. I wrote Richard, giving the wrong time and day to meet at the station. I made certain I intercepted most of the letters after the first one. Hannah suspected what I was doing, but I lied several times to my family, saying Richard didn't really care about any of us and that he stood Daed up at the station."

"We saw Richard waiting outside the café," Debbie said. "He must have wanted to meet you." She remembered the sad sight of Richard sitting alone, occasionally glancing at his watch.

Benjamin reached for his sister's hand. "I do not want you to hate me, not the way Dawdi hated his flesh and blood. If Richard truly wants half of the business, then so be it. I am very sorry for all I have done."

Hannah threw her arms around her brother's neck with a sob. "I could never hate you, Benjamin. I am so glad you and Daed no longer carry this burden. It is better to forgive and seek forgiveness. Why not make amends with Richard, ja?"

Ian's eyes appeared suspiciously moist as he watched the siblings reconcile. "It's not a crime to burn old letters, unless they're addressed to someone else. But I hope you reach out to Richard. You might find some additional answers to your family history. For now, I see no reason to intervene in family matters, and I wish each of you the best."

Debbie appreciated Ian's tact, but she had a few further questions to explore. She faced Benjamin. "Can you help us settle a few problems? I saw you near the Good Shepherd, where Eileen lives. She initially thought you were Samuel."

Despite Hannah's arm about his shoulders for support, Benjamin wilted as he studied the floor. "Ja, I drove past the Good Shepherd. I wondered who Eileen might be, what kind of woman she was, to so completely change Samuel's mind. It is no small thing to leave the Amish. I never meant to frighten her. Dawdi told us terrible things about her too. Like Daed, I wondered if Dawdi had not been wholly truthful with me years ago."

Debbie folded her arms across her chest. "My employee, Annie, says her brother thought he saw you driving out of Buona Vita late at night. Someone tried to break into his restaurant. Nothing stolen, but Ricky needed to fix a window."

Benjamin blanched as he disentangled from his sister's embrace. "I have been working on furniture every night for the past two weeks, including the order for a friend of yours, Becky Thomas. Daed hired other men, Amish of course, from the Sugarcreek community to work alongside me. They can verify my whereabouts."

"Annie said the buggy had a broken reflector. I noticed yours was new. Did you replace it this past week?"

Benjamin frowned, his brows dipping. "Ne, my buggy has had a new reflector since Independence Day. The last I checked, it is still there at the back of the buggy."

"Perhaps your employee is mistaken," Daniel said, his voice grim. "I cannot speak for all our young men, but it is dangerous to drive in the night on a poorly lit street. We try to avoid that if we can, especially in busy areas with speeding cars. Too much risk of an accident."

# CHAPTER THIRTY-THREE

*D*ebbie held her breath as she and Janet waited in the car while Ian pulled into a concrete driveway webbed with cracks. Unlike the Lapps' home, Annie's family residence appeared small and shabby, surrounded by weeds bursting with seed. By now the sun was a ball of fire, sinking past the tree line, but not even the beauty of a sunset could hide the decay of the home and the yard surrounded by a collapsing fence. Junk peeked from behind an open gate, including an antique stove now covered in rust.

How could anyone not feel sad for Annie? The house, likely once a cute cottage, now had a brown shutter hanging sideways. A few windows had lost their shutters altogether. The puce-colored siding needed to be scraped and freshly painted.

A thin man, balding and wearing a pair of red shorts and a tight black muscle shirt, opened the door after Ian knocked a third time. Debbie couldn't hear the conversation, but it was evident that neither Annie nor Nicholas was home. At first, Ian refused to budge, but finally he conceded, and the man slammed the door shut, rattling an ancient Christmas wreath long past its prime, the red poinsettias now a sickly pink.

"I didn't know Annie lived in such a house," Debbie admitted, her heart aching for the young woman. How had she and Janet missed this? Was this the reason for Annie's delay into college? Finances and a possibly rough family situation? Guilt slithered through her as she studied the grounds a second time.

Ian approached Janet's side of the car. She lowered the window, and Debbie leaned over the armrest to hear better.

"It appears Annie and her brother Nicholas are at the movies."

"Which theater?" Janet asked.

Ian sighed as he rubbed the back of his neck. "The Quaker Theater in New Philly. Their dad says they left immediately after Annie got off work."

He rested his palm against the hood of Janet's car. "I'm going to have to question Nicholas tomorrow regarding this phantom Amish buggy."

"Annie said she's heading to college soon. Her quitting date just moved up a few days," Debbie said, recalling her previous conversation with Annie. Why had her plans changed in such a hurry? Something had troubled the young woman during her phone call at the café. Chronic stress didn't always lead to the best choices.

Debbie had been wrong about Benjamin and had assumed the worst. Could she be wrong about Annie as well?

# CHAPTER THIRTY-FOUR

Monday morning came far too early, signaled by the incessant beep of the alarm clock on the nightstand. Debbie swung her feet off the bed and pounded the button on her clock. Gray dawn barely filtered through the curtains. She got ready for her day, bypassing the pressed blouses and billowy cardigans and settling for dressing in a T-shirt as Janet often did. The train station logo felt appropriate with the khaki pants. When she peered into her bathroom mirror, she winced at the sight of dark, puffy circles beneath her eyes.

Honestly, she dreaded this morning. She'd endured yet another sleepless night, worrying about Annie, Eileen, Richard, and the café. She padded downstairs and slipped her feet into her sneakers. A ding echoed from her cell phone. When she retrieved it, shock rippled through her with what she read.

The evening before, Debbie had texted her old college friend, Abigail Messener, regarding Annie's start date at Ohio State. As dean for the Liberal Arts Department, Abigail would hopefully be able to provide answers. Debbie had offered to connect Annie with Abigail, but Annie had refused.

Abigail had returned the text at midnight.

DEBBIE, YOU MUST UNDERSTAND THAT I CANNOT SHARE PERSONAL INFORMATION ABOUT OUR STUDENTS. THE ONLY THING I

CAN TELL YOU IS THAT YOU NEED TO ASK ANNIE WHY SHE'S NOT ATTENDING OHIO STATE. HOPEFULLY, SHE WILL TELL YOU THE TRUTH, AS UNPLEASANT AS IT IS. I DO FEEL I SHOULD WARN YOU TO THINK TWICE BEFORE YOU TRUST HER IN ANY POSITION OF RESPONSIBILITY.

Debbie sank onto her bed, numb inside. So there *was* a reason why Annie was being so evasive about attending the university.

A deep chill settled in her as she contemplated Annie's extraordinary helpfulness, her constant willingness to stay late at the café, and her ability to hop into a conversation effortlessly, as if she had listened to every detail. Then there was Annie's brother, who lied about Benjamin—or was that Annie lying?

For all the grace Debbie had extended, she needed to have another conversation with her young employee. Or would the term *confrontation* be more accurate? But first, she needed to call Janet.

Debbie's heart pounded erratically as she drove to Annie's house on Wilson Street. The gray dawn had warmed to faint tones of pink. Before leaving her house, she had left a detailed phone message for Janet, telling her what Abigail had said. Perhaps it was risky to confront Annie alone, but Debbie dared not wait another second. Not when Annie had hinted that she would end work soon. Plus, Ian more than likely had his hands full this morning.

Debbie left a message for Janet of the plan to drive to Annie's house. The rest of the plan? Well, she'd have to see how this conversation played out.

Debbie pulled up opposite Annie's house. To her shock, a figure exited a side door wearing a large black hooded sweatshirt, hiding both form and face. He or she ducked into the familiar yellow Corvette and eased out of the driveway, heading in the opposite direction of Debbie's car.

Was that Annie inside the Corvette? If so, she was headed south of the train depot. Should Debbie follow the car and see where it was headed? And who might be driving?

Inhaling sharply, she eased on the gas pedal and followed the car, keeping the taillights in view. Better not look like she was following too close and arouse suspicion. Her phone rang, the sound jarring. The flashing screen revealed Janet's number. Debbie pressed the button on her steering wheel and didn't even manage to utter a hello before her friend cut in.

"Don't you dare do anything without me, Debbie Albright," Janet's voice warned from the other end. "I just tried to call Ian. It went straight to his voice mail. He left over an hour ago, rushing off to a truck accident. And someone broke into Northside Auto Repair. I heard it over the police radio around three this morning. I'm at the café now, but I can meet you."

Debbie scanned the road. "I don't have time to wait for you. Either Annie or Nicholas left the house before I could get out of the car, and I'm following to see where they're headed. It could be Annie. I'm sure she must have learned by now that Ian has more questions for her. I don't want her to slip away before someone has a chance to talk with her. Besides, you can track me on my phone, right? Check the GPS and see where I'm headed? As soon as I can, I'll send my location to you."

"I don't like this. Not one bit." Janet sounded worried.

"I don't either. The Corvette is headed out of town, Janet. Turning on South Sixth Street. Gotta go."

She ended the call. If that was Annie, she wasn't on her way to work.

Blowing out a harsh breath, Debbie managed to follow the Corvette at a discreet distance. However, traffic remained light, and she feared she'd be noticed. A few minutes later, the car turned onto Moravian Trail Road. By now, Debbie was outside Dennison. Trees and the occasional farmstead provided the only view. The Corvette made a swift left turn into one such farmstead.

All at once, realization sank into Debbie. This was Annie's grandfather's farm, where Nicholas occasionally helped. Debbie slowed her car, hoping that whoever drove the sports car wouldn't notice her. The driver parked beside a small house and a storage shed with doors gaping wide open.

The black-hooded figure hopped out of the car, opened the trunk, and pushed the sweatshirt hood back, revealing a long swath of pale blond hair. *Annie.* The young woman leaned into the trunk, rummaging through items.

Debbie had every intention of driving past the farm, but the sight of that long blond hair prompted a split-second decision. She stopped the car, sent a quick text to Janet, and then pulled into the driveway, fully aware the sound of gravel crunching beneath her tires would give her away. But Annie appeared to be alone, and Debbie wanted answers.

She climbed out of the car. Annie had retrieved a cardboard box from the trunk before she spun around to see Debbie approaching her.

"Debbie! What are you doing here? You scared me." Annie offered a weak smile. "Good morning."

"Hey, yourself. I thought I'd swing by and see how you're doing, but then I saw you leave the house and followed you. Did you get any sleep last night? You look pretty tired."

Shadows curved beneath Annie's eyes. "I slept some."

Steeling herself, Debbie decided to plunge in before she lost any courage. "I got a text from my friend Abigail at Ohio State. She told me to ask you why you weren't registering for classes. Please, Annie, won't you trust me with the truth?"

Annie clutched the box closer to her chest. "I couldn't register, because I lost my scholarship. I worked too many jobs, trying to afford college, and hurt my grade-point average. I don't have enough money to enroll again. I guess I was so embarrassed by my failure, I hid it."

Debbie sighed. Was she only going to get partial truths? This couldn't be what Abigail had hinted at. "Annie, do you know something about the antiques taken from Kim? Silas said he saw someone wearing a sweatshirt like yours trying to enter the museum late at night. He said someone ran away fast, and you mentioned one day that you'd gone to college on a track scholarship. What you just told me isn't the whole truth, is it? There's another reason you didn't apply for classes."

Annie froze, the color draining from her face. "All lies. My history professor never liked me, and she accused me of plagiarism. She has no proof, and I've been trying to clear my name, but no one will believe me." She scowled and said bitterly, "They took away my scholarship, and now the mark is on my permanent record, so I can't even transfer to another school."

Debbie strove to keep her voice calm. "Someone took the missing kitchen antiques from Kim's office. I suspect that same person was almost caught by Silas in the Pullman car and abandoned them in their haste to escape."

Annie's eyes rounded. "You think I did that?"

Debbie held her hands out. "Chief Shaw wants to know what's going on. He's ready for some answers. Kim placed additional video cameras all over the station. We didn't tell anyone when they were installed. But we saw you on the feed, wearing that same black sweatshirt you're wearing now."

For a moment, Debbie feared the young woman might bolt. And although Debbie wore comfortable clothes and sneakers, she had no desire to tackle or be tackled by Annie should the occasion arise.

Annie's bottom lip trembled. "No one gives the Butler kids a second chance. Everyone assumes the worst about Nicholas and me. Besides, tons of kids wear black sweatshirts."

She might have believed Annie's act, if several glaring facts didn't remain.

"What about Benjamin? You've tried repeatedly to implicate an innocent man for the break-in at Buona Vita. That wasn't the truth, was it?"

Annie opened her mouth. She stepped backward, her gaze darting away from Debbie. "You should leave."

Debbie followed Annie's furtive gaze to the remaining cardboard box in the opened trunk of the car. A yellow tray peeked out of the box, along with a framed photo. A sick feeling settled over her.

"Annie, you can't lie to me anymore. I see my grandmother's tray in your trunk. I'd guess you have the items from Kim's desk too. Why would you do something like that to us?"

Annie swallowed hard. "I hoped the history department would reconsider once they learned of the Unnamed Soldier and the connection to the Dennison station. I've worked hard for my degree. What happened wasn't fair."

Debbie shook her head. "That doesn't justify your thefts."

Annie's expression flattened. "I needed the money after losing my scholarships. My loans are the only thing I have left, and they're not enough. Kim was going to put those pieces in a museum and let them gather dust, but I know what they're worth. She left her office door open most of the time, making it easy for me to slip in and put things in my backpack. If Kim really cared about this stuff, she would have locked her door."

At last, the truth from Annie. Debbie blew out a frustrated breath. "The tray is sentimental to my family and worth far more than the cash it would bring by selling it. My mom donated it to the café to bless others. And Kim trusted all of us to do the right thing and leave her office alone."

Fingers dug into Debbie's shoulder, forcing her to whirl around to face a young man with blond hair. So engrossed in confronting Annie, Debbie hadn't heard his approach.

Nicholas's icy gaze bored into hers. He loomed over Debbie, his grip tight. He wore a light denim jacket, his left pocket bulging. With what? Hopefully not a weapon.

"Annie, I told you stealing from the depot was a dumb idea. You swore no one would catch you…" He caught Debbie's glance at his jacket pocket and took a menacing step forward. "What are you looking at?"

Debbie held her tongue. If she could just make a run for her car, she could lock the door and speed away.

Annie's face contorted, the innocent expression completely lost. "Stop it, Nicholas. Stop talking."

Nicholas stared at Debbie. "What are we going to do with her?"

Annie hissed as she rubbed her arms. "I told you to stop talking. Let me think a minute. I wasn't counting on seeing her today. This ruins everything."

Unsure if he could truly hurt her or not with whatever was in his pocket, Debbie took a hesitant step toward her car. He startled, reached out, and grabbed her arm. She kicked his shin as hard as she could, satisfied when he grunted. His hand, however, remained like a vise curled around her elbow.

"You're not going anywhere." He grabbed her phone from where it peeked out of her back pocket and pushed her roughly in the direction of the shed, thrusting her inside before slamming the doors. The sound of a bar sliding to lock her inside the cramped building made her stomach roil. She hated enclosed spaces.

A tiny window splotched with grime offered dim light, revealing stacked boxes of items, including a few stuffed with automobile parts. Kim's missing antiques gleamed from another open box. She could only hope Janet would find her location via GPS. Meanwhile, the siblings argued outside the shed.

"*You* ruined everything." Nicholas raised his voice. "We had a good thing going until you got the job at the café. You just had to steal from the depot. All because of your stupid degree and student loans and your crazy ego. I warned you it wouldn't be worth the risk or the payback."

"Shut up—she'll hear you. You weren't so smooth at Buona Vita or the auto store either. But I got some good stuff. You think I can pay off my loans with a minimum-wage job? I need lots of money, and fast."

"I'm not covering for you anymore. There's no way the school is gonna take you back after all you've done. And you said yourself you'll never get into another college or university again. Not after all your cheating."

"Like you have a right to talk to me about cheating when you've been stealing ever since Mom died."

Sorrow filled Debbie. How tragic for both kids to have made such bad choices and at such a young age. Despite her compassion for them both, she didn't want to stick around and see what happened next. Who knew what desperation might drive both of the Butlers to do? She eased toward the window. It would be a tight squeeze, but she might be able to wiggle through if she tried. Besides, the bolted door was the only other exit.

She pulled on the latch of the window to no avail. Unfortunately, paint sealed it shut. Running her fingers around the frame, she searched for a crack. Could she free the window from the paint and open it? Might Annie have taken a knife from Kim's office, or something sharp? Debbie moved to the nearest box of antiques, rummaging through the contents. Hadn't Kim shared that a silver cutlery set had been taken? Debbie's fingers grazed a knife. She picked it up and began to work on the thick paint coating the warped window frame.

Meanwhile, the Butler kids argued louder and louder, with Annie suggesting they flee town altogether and leave Debbie to swelter in the shed.

"You can't be serious, Annie. We can't just leave her in there!" Nicholas protested, sounding anxious.

Annie moaned. "I never meant for this to happen. I don't know what to do."

Debbie gulped before turning her attention to the window. Her hand shook as she gripped the knife. She gritted her teeth and attacked the window frame again just as red and blue lights flashed into the shed, signaling rescue.

# CHAPTER THIRTY-FIVE

*A*fter reading their Miranda rights and assisting Annie and Nicholas into the squad car, Ian came over to talk to Debbie. "You all right? Next time, promise me that you'll wait for me, okay?"

Debbie nodded, relieved to have her friends close to her again.

Annie wept as she sat in the back of the car, as helpless as could be. She refused to look at either Janet or Debbie. Nicholas hung his head as he sat beside his sister.

"I do feel sorry for Annie, despite her steady stream of lies about Benjamin," Janet said. "She's had a rough life. It's a shame the Butler kids enabled each other to such a degree." Debbie watched as Ian slid into the car and headed toward the road. "Part of me is angry too. Annie would have framed Benjamin without a second thought."

"She saw Benjamin as an easy target, and with our conversations so out in the open, she saw an opportunity and took it." Debbie watched the cruiser exit the farmstead. "But you're right. Lies only make bigger messes. At some point, she'll need to learn that lesson before it further damages her life."

"Maybe we need to be more careful in the future," Janet said. "Dennison might be a small community, but you never fully know someone's heart until the pressure comes. Time has a way of revealing truth, doesn't it?"

Yes, it did.

Janet patted Debbie's shoulder. "I'm going to whip us up a couple of sugary mocha lattes at the café. I think you and I both need a good, long break."

An hour later Debbie stood outside the café, grateful for the resolution. Her grandmother's beloved tray was back in the Whistle Stop Café where it belonged. She held one of Janet's mocha confections, the flavor and warmth soothing. Life would return to normal again.

It had been quite a risk confronting Annie. If only Debbie had spoken with her sooner, but perhaps fear had kept her from a tough conversation.

The morning sun and the birds awakening with song brought a measure of comfort, slowing her racing heartbeat to a manageable level. A familiar red truck pulled into the parking lot. Hammer barked as soon as he saw Debbie. Greg got out of the truck, wearing a denim jacket thrown over a white T-shirt. Today, he wore a pair of rugged cowboy boots with his jeans. A nice look, if she was honest with herself. Somehow, he managed to end up at the café when she needed him the most.

He reached her side, standing with her as they surveyed the parking lot together. "I ran into Ian. I heard about Annie and Nicholas. I'm sorry."

"I guess Annie wasn't what she seemed. I'm rarely hoodwinked by people, so this is humbling, for sure. It appears she and her brother ramped up the crime, emboldened by each act. I feel so bad for both of them, especially knowing what kind of home they came from. Part of me feels foolish for trusting her as much as I did."

"You've got a generous heart, Debbie. Don't change because of one broken person or a painful circumstance."

She knew Greg spoke from experience, especially as a widower. Despite life's shifting circumstances, he was one of the most content friends she had ever encountered.

He continued. "I know the situation surrounding Eileen's 'Dear Jane' letter, and I can understand how that's been especially trying for you."

Debbie studied her sneakers. "It's been difficult, digging into Eileen's story and seeing the loss she experienced. She's done so well, despite all she went through. I admire her spirit and courage. I want to be more like her—not held back by painful experiences. Finding joy in life, no matter where the twisting path leads. That's what Eileen has done."

Her body shook, nearly to the point of her teeth chattering, and it was August. Yes, fear had followed her, if she was truthful. She felt that bubbling stress inside of her—that desire to control the outcome and make everything perfect. But life wasn't perfect. She had learned that when she moved to the city to be closer to Reed, and later when she lost him in Afghanistan.

Debbie realized she stood rather close to Greg. He smiled at her, and he didn't make a move to step backward after he placed his jacket over her shoulders. A whiff of masculine spice and musk teased her nose. He smelled good.

She shivered again. "Thank you for being here and listening."

A pensive look crossed his face, dimming the smile a notch. "You know, it's okay to say goodbye to the past. We give thanks for the beauty and the wonder we experienced. I'm grateful, despite every painful trial I've gone through. Each circumstance has drawn me closer to God. I've learned to look forward to something new each day. Different, but no less beautiful."

She pulled the denim jacket tighter around herself, warding against the chill inside. Somehow, the conversation had shifted from Eileen to her, and she wasn't sure what to make of it. She strove to lighten the mood. "If you'd like to try something new, I'll bring the Yuanyang next time."

"The what?" He frowned.

"A Yuanyang is Janet's latest coffee obsession. It's an espresso mixed with milk tea. It's actually really good."

He raised an eyebrow, nonplussed by her weak attempt at humor to diffuse the heavy topic at hand. "Are you inviting me for coffee?"

"Uh—maybe."

He smiled in the most charming way. "Yuanyang it is. My offer to be a guinea pig still stands. Coffee, kuchen, whoopie pies, crazy coffee, you name it. When you need me, I'll be there."

There it was—Greg's quiet declaration of friendship and total acceptance. During her twenty years of city living, she had too often felt alone. Sure, she had friends in the city, but she had still felt isolated sometimes. Now, in Dennison, friends surrounded her. She relaxed as she stuck her hands in the roomy jacket pockets. "Janet has plenty of plans for the bakery. I can hardly keep up with her menu, and when your mom returns from vacation, we'll have a blast in the kitchen as we always do. Did I tell you Janet's finally mastered the kuchen?"

"I can't wait to try it." He chuckled.

"Would you like your jacket back?" She raised one long sleeve hiding her hand.

His grin widened. "No, you keep it. I'll get it another day."

Debbie was sitting in a booth with Janet and Kim after the café closed, when Kim's cell phone rang. She answered it and after a moment said, "Of course you can come. Why not make the Whistle Stop Café the meeting place? Yes, we'll wait for you." She hung up, her expression bemused. "Richard Brown says he's finally ready to meet. He wants to visit this Sunday."

"He wants to meet with the Lapp family?" Debbie blinked with surprise.

"No, not this trip. I think he feels skittish about his Amish relatives, considering the previous rejection. Instead, he wants to meet my mom, and he's got something to show us."

# CHAPTER THIRTY-SIX

On Sunday after church, the train station lay empty. Blissfully quiet. Debbie paced the sidewalk while Kim and Janet sat on the benches positioned at the platform.

Kim glanced at her watch several times, and her foot tapped a rhythm, hinting at her nervousness. No sign of Richard Brown.

Janet shielded her eyes against the sun. "I hope we don't get a storm later. This humidity feels like rain coming."

Kim studied the few clouds floating overhead. "I hope not. I want smooth travels for our mysterious gentleman. Not one excuse for him to avoid meeting us. I think we've all waited long enough."

Debbie stood when she saw a black car enter the parking lot. Her stomach fluttered in anticipation. At long last, she would finally meet the elusive Mr. Brown. "He's here."

The Jaguar purred, coming to a stop in front of the station. A man lingered inside the car, as if bolstering courage. Then he got out and came toward them. Dressed in navy slacks with a collared shirt trimmed with a crisp tie, he stopped when Debbie's friends joined her.

"Welcome," Kim said to him. "We've got some coffee and baked goods inside the café. Janet's pretty famous for her cinnamon buns."

He approached them, hesitant, with a leather briefcase in hand. On closer look, Richard's eyes were indeed a vibrant green. His hair wasn't as fair as Benjamin Lapp's, but the resemblance was strong. Square jaw. Thick brows. Straight nose. His physique, although trim, didn't evidence the hard labor of the local Lapp men. Instead, he appeared more the scholar.

Richard held out a hand, which Debbie and her friends promptly shook in turn.

"I must apologize for the delay in responding. But if you have an hour, I can explain everything," he said quietly.

Inside the café, after Janet had served coffee and cinnamon buns, which Richard didn't touch, he spoke. "I know you must have questions, and I'll answer them after I share about my father and the letter I left at the lamppost. I'm not surprised you couldn't find him easily. He didn't want to be found. My father had several identities. You might have known him as Samuel Lapp. I knew him as Samuel Brown. And the world knew him as the Unnamed Soldier, an intrepid journalist, and finally as Gavin McAllister, a famous author."

"Gavin McAllister?" Kim exclaimed, her eyes nearly bulging. "He wrote *Moon Over Boston*, *Rebecca's Orchard*, and so many other famous stories."

Richard loosened the knot of his tie before clearing his throat. "Yes, he's best known for his lighthearted novels. He didn't want to bring the darkness of the world into people's homes. As a result, his fiction sold very well."

"How did you learn about Daniel and Benjamin?" Debbie asked.

"I didn't know my father was Amish until I was an adult although, in hindsight, I'm not sure why it didn't register sooner. He refused photos. He lived simply on a farmstead outside New York City, close enough to his publisher but far away from the noise of the city. He married a nurse he met in the hospital after he was injured at Iwo Jima, and when they married, he chose her last name, claiming he had lost everything back home. My mom is still alive. Her name is Clarice. It's been hard for her since my dad died a little over a year ago."

Richard picked up his fork and put it down again before continuing. "When my father and I had heart-to-heart conversations, he spoke of a wonderful stationmaster and how she changed his life. He credited her for sparking his interest in writing. But his injury to his leg kept him rather immobile. I think he feared he would be a burden to her, especially since Eileen had a father to take care of as well. As I said, my mother was a nurse during the war and helped him recover from his injury. A natural homebody, she never left his side."

He turned to Debbie. "When you answered my phone call that day, I froze. I heard you speak with an Eileen, and I knew it was the Eileen who had affected my father so greatly. Unfortunately, my mother walked into the room right then. I didn't want her to overhear my conversation. She didn't know I had stumbled across my father's correspondence with another former Amish man, Frank Raber. My father kept those letters hidden in his desk. They surprised me with yet another mysterious layer of the man I loved.

"In the letters, my father mentioned a brother—a Jacob Lapp, and a nephew, Daniel. At some point, he gave up trying to reach his family, especially after being shunned. Truthfully, my father had changed so much from the war, he could no longer return to Dennison. I hoped Jacob's son, Daniel, would prove different from Jacob, but I was wrong."

"You might find things could change in the future. The Lapps were afraid you would claim part ownership to their lumberyard." Debbie's heart ached for the visible pain playing across Richard's face.

He fiddled with the fork, still avoiding the dessert. "As you can see, I'm not struggling for money. I'm an investor, and I took my father's fortune and grew it. I have no need for more money or more conflict in my life. I just wanted to learn about my roots."

"How did you come across your father's letter to Eileen?" Janet asked.

"I found it one day when I was going through his old uniforms," Richard said. "He hung them in the attic decades ago and had made my mother promise to never mention them again. After he died, my mom asked me to do something with them. The letter to Eileen was in one of the jacket pockets."

"I'm surprised you didn't open it," Debbie said. "I don't know if I would have been that conscientious."

"It had the address," Richard said. "That's all I needed. What was inside wasn't for my eyes. And when no one met me at the train station, I left it there, praying that if God wanted Eileen to have it, the right person would come along." He shrugged. "I wasn't even sure if she was still alive."

After a moment of silence, Kim pushed her half-eaten cinnamon bun to the side. "I understand Frank might have saved Samuel's life at Iwo Jima," she said. "It's strange—my father survived Iwo Jima as well. His name was Rafe Palmer. He carried a half-unconscious man over his shoulder through enemy fire. He left the man with a medic and drew enemy fire away to save their lives. He won a medal for those actions."

Debbie and Janet stared at each other in amazement. It hadn't occurred to Debbie that, with the excitement surrounding Annie's arrest, she hadn't told Kim about the contents of Frank Raber's letter to Samuel. If she had, they could have put the puzzle pieces together sooner.

Richard dropped his fork with a clatter, disbelief shining in his eyes. "My father said a stranger carried him through gunfire, straight to the care of Frank Raber, who was a medic."

# CHAPTER THIRTY-SEVEN

*Dennison, Ohio*
*October 1946*

*Eileen leaned against the kitchen wall, her cheeks aching from continually smiling. Regardless of the state of her facial muscles, her heart sang. Rafe's new house rang with laughter and celebration. For the past year, he had worked hard, helping raise some of the prettiest homes in the community. Endless hours in the sun had bronzed his skin with a marvelous glow. In his spare time, he mentored returning veterans, offering a hearty meal and work to those who didn't know how to begin life again, even those whose hands shook from the war. Anyone could hold a hammer or paintbrush in Rafe's growing business.*

*Today, he had invited Eileen and her father to celebrate the purchase of his first home and to meet his* mother, Maria, who had finally moved all the way from Little Italy, New York.

Eileen felt both the heady joy and the seriousness of the celebration. Rafe would never leave Dennison. He was intent on proving it to her every chance he had.

When he had shared his plans to buy the charming craftsman-style house, he had winked at her. "See? You'll never get rid of me."

Alberto and his family had crowded into the newly painted kitchen, bringing fragrant dishes of lasagna and tiramisu to share. Bottles of tart lemonade and bowls of knotted garlic rolls soon cluttered the kitchen table. Someone started the record player, the initial static of the needle hitting vinyl soon replaced with boisterous singing. Rafe's doing, she guessed. Soon the house was filled with the sounds of big band music.

"You'll scare the neighbors with this racket!" Alberto cried as he slapped Rafe on the back. Rafe shrugged, but he caught Eileen's gaze. In fact, all evening, it seemed he couldn't look away.

She poured herself a glass of lemonade, enjoying Alberto's young daughter demonstrating the latest dance moves in the living room, her white bobby socks helping her slide across the varnished hardwood floor.

Eileen laughed with everyone in the room. Her papa had made a rare appearance tonight, sitting on the couch beside Rafe's petite mother, Maria, with her rolled chignon and string of pearls. She beamed with a sweet expression as Eileen's father tapped his feet to the rhythm. She had never seen him so happy. His cheeks flushed bright. In the days to come, she would try to get him out of the house more often, and certainly, playing music seemed to help whenever he became frustrated. The Carosi family had adopted her and her father, treating them like close kin.

Never had she felt such a sense of belonging as she did with them.

Alberto joined Eileen and raised his lemonade in toast. She raised her glass, clinking it with his. "You must be so proud of your nephew."

Alberto sighed, though it was of pure contentment. "I've always been proud of Rafe. When his father died, I thought of him as my own. After he went to war with all the rest, particularly fighting in the Pacific, I feared I would never see him again."

She held her glass close to her chest, choosing to keep silent and learn more. Alberto glanced at her and then pointed his half-empty glass toward a built-in shelf where a small cedar box perched beside a miniature globe. "Do you know what's inside that box?"

She shook her head, her earrings bouncing.

*"Ask Rafe. Ask him to tell you the full story about the medal inside. It's a Navy Cross."*

*She wanted to probe further, but Alberto pushed away from the wall and danced toward his daughter, bringing a fresh round of laughter throughout the living room.*

*Rafe joined her. "I don't suppose I could talk you into the jitterbug or the Charleston, could I?"*

*She smiled. "Maybe. A walk might be nice. Or just sitting on the front porch. Alone."*

*His eyes widened, and he took her hand and led her away from the not-so-secret smiles of the Carosi family. Out on the porch, they sat together on the steps while the moon hung like a silver coin in the twilight sky.*

*"Alberto told me to ask you about the box on your shelf."*

*He tensed beside her. "Oh?"*

*"Why didn't you tell me?" She nudged his shoulder with her own, keeping her voice light.*

*He rubbed the back of his neck as if embarrassed. "There's not much to say. I carried an injured man through enemy territory during a banzai attack. The Japanese had infiltrated our area of the mountain at Iwo Jima, but a few of us evaded capture at the last minute. Got this lovely eyebrow, which you can see, thanks to a bullet whizzing past. That volcanic sand was so thick, most of us sank to our calves when we first landed on the island. When I finally broke free of the sand with my comrade and, because of providence, found a medic crouching next to a captured foxhole—a hole big enough for a few men to hide inside, I offered to draw away enemy fire while the medic bandaged the marine I had carried. The guy I saved—I never got his name. He was bleeding pretty heavy by the time I reached the medic, and I—"*

*Rafe stopped midsentence, still rubbing his neck.*

*"You're a hero!" she blurted. "And yet you tell no one. Why?"*

*Beneath the mellow porch light, his Adam's apple bobbed as he cleared his throat. "My mother taught me to keep such things quiet, I guess. Kinda ruins the giving, don't you think? Especially if one insists on the entire world knowing every detail."*

*Her gaze flitted over his face, lingering at the faint white line on his temple. His sleeves were rolled up, and in the pale light, he folded his muscular arms across his chest. Arms that had helped rebuild Dennison and somehow carried a fallen soldier through a danger-infested island.*

*She had always wondered about the story behind his service. How wonderfully humble. "You fought in* the Pacific and endured one of the most important and deadly battles our troops ever faced. Do you want to talk about it?"

Rafe reached over and captured her hand, entwining his fingers with hers. "No, Eileen. I don't. It's enough being here with you. I thank God every day for the extra time He has allowed me. I've found you. I have a family again. I don't want to relive the past when there's so much living to do."

She gripped his hand, her fingers meshed with his. So Rafe had fought at Iwo Jima, in one of the fiercest battles on record. When the marines captured the mountain, a photographer snapped the iconic moment of the weary soldiers raising the flag. Many men had perished along the broken path leading to the peak. A prayer of thanksgiving rose within her, for both Rafe and the brave men who had survived with him. The miracle of Rafe sitting beside her brought fresh tears to her eyes.

Sultry tunes filtered through the open window while crickets chirped in unison. Rafe clasped her hand, gently tugging her to her feet to dance on the lawn. "When I'm with you, I feel as though I can do anything. I don't see an awful past. Instead, I see a beautiful future with the two of us together. We can hike in the Grand Canyon, find a jazz band in New

*York City or the French quarter in New Orleans. We can tour the Badlands in South Dakota and listen to the coyotes howl while hiking near Mount Rushmore, or we can slip across the border to Montreal and speak bad French while eating chocolate-stuffed croissants. See, I've even practiced.* Je t'aime."

*She placed a finger against his lips. He waited, and when her hand dropped, he pulled her close and rested his head against hers.*

*"Live a little, Eileen," he whispered. "We only have one life. Don't you get a second chance at happiness too?" His breath was warm against her ear.*

*She pressed her lips together. Why should she carry this weight of grief forever? Would she allow hollow loneliness and disappointment and fear to define her for the rest of her years? Samuel was never coming back, and it was time she accepted it. Besides, she couldn't, didn't want to imagine her life without Rafe. A deep shuddering breath escaped her, while Vera Lynn crooned in the background, her voice mingling with the music of crickets.*

*She tilted her head to look up at Rafe. "What did you just say to me? You know—the French part?"*

*His mouth tilted at the corner, relief flooding his expression as he twirled her to the music. "I said I love you."*

She stumbled in the damp grass as his left arm swept behind her, pulling her upright and close to him. Her heart nearly burst with joy as she finally surrendered to the music, to the moment, and to him. The melting kiss that followed...

What could she say to do it justice?

"I think it's my turn, Mr. Palmer," she said with a grin while rehearsing the precious words in her head, now seared into her heart and soul. As carefully and as gently as she could, she repeated, "Je t'aime."

# CHAPTER THIRTY-EIGHT

*L*ater on Sunday afternoon, Debbie, Janet, Kim, and Richard arrived at Eileen's tiny apartment at Good Shepherd. He tugged again at his tie, something Debbie now recognized to be a nervous habit.

"You are Samuel's boy. I can see it. How wonderful." Eileen's warm welcome appeared to set him at ease. He shared his story, including what he told Debbie and her friends.

Instead of grief, Eileen appeared delighted. Debbie watched in amazement as Eileen reached out her frail hands to clasp Richard's.

He took a deep breath as he squeezed her hands in return. "Did you know your husband, Rafe, saved my father's life?"

"No," she whispered, her eyes widening as she continued to hold Richard's hands. "How incredible. Rafe never knew the name of the man."

"We didn't figure it out either until just now," Debbie added, "when we were talking with Kim about rescue stories at Iwo Jima. It appears Samuel and your Rafe found each other during the battle, even if for a moment in time. I wouldn't believe it if I wasn't convinced that God loves to amaze us." She touched Eileen's arm. "Someday soon we'll tell you the rest of that incredible story."

Richard blinked away a tear as he finally let go of Eileen's hands. He cleared his throat, his voice thick when he spoke. "I came to find family and thought they didn't care for me. But it turns out, I found family regardless."

"My sweet boy, God works in mysterious ways. You would have done my Rafe's heart a world of good if he could have seen you sitting beside me. He never wanted to talk about the battles. He said there was too much living to do, and you are proof of that. Sometimes the most beautiful sunsets are the ones that come after the storm. I can rest knowing Samuel found his place of belonging and safety after all."

Richard pulled a book out of his briefcase. The thick volume had a vintage cover in pristine condition. "My father always wanted you to have this story. He wrote it for you. My mother understood who you were to him and the impact you had on his life. She was such a quiet woman, shy and reserved. They met when she was a nurse and he a patient due to a wound in his leg. When he became the famous Gavin McAllister, she was so proud of him. I remember them sitting in a pair of wingback chairs next to the fireplace. They would read together and discuss books. She was always the first person to read his work. He dedicated plenty of novels to her, but this one was always intended for you. I think it might have been his best work. He wanted you to know how grateful he was for your friendship. I can't help but think he worried about you, whether or not you were happy."

Eileen took the book. The cover depicted the painted silhouette of a couple walking along a country road lined with wildflowers. *We'll Meet Again*. She opened it and traced the print along the dust jacket, perhaps searching for a photo, but, as with the Unnamed Soldier articles, Samuel had preferred to remain hidden.

Eileen adjusted her glasses, the gold frames winking in the light while the chains attached to each side quivered about her face. "'Dedicated to E. May there always be a song in your heart. Thank you for your friendship. Because of you, I took the path less traveled.'"

Richard gestured at the volume. "The story of a soldier returning to his sweetheart after a long absence rose to the top of the best-seller lists. He worked on it for years and finally released it in 1956. He published over forty books, but this remained one of his favorites, and one of his bestselling novels. He said he wouldn't have had the courage to write if it hadn't been for you lighting the fire. Your support of his dreams meant the world to him."

Eileen laughed through her tears. "I didn't read much all those years ago. Too busy! I know I'll enjoy the novel. I'm thrilled Samuel found someone who complemented him so well."

"My mother really did. She was heartbroken when he passed a year ago." He ducked his head. "I'm sorry it took me so long to get this letter to you. I was afraid to find out what my father left behind all those years ago."

Debbie released a pent-up breath. Richard's humble admission struck something inside her. Hadn't fear ruled her these past few weeks? When dealing with Annie, when managing the café, and when running into Greg, who had offered friendship?

Everyone had tears in their eyes when Richard said his last goodbye. Janet and Kim walked with him to the reception area while Debbie remained with Eileen in the small apartment. Her throat tightened as she watched the older woman caress the pages of the novel.

Eileen raised her head, her gaze piercing. "I know you've experienced loss, Debbie."

Debbie shifted uncomfortably in the rocking chair. "I thought I had managed the grief of losing my fiancé, but the last few days… Well, it's done something to me, and I've felt the grief again."

"Grief doesn't come all at once. It comes in cycles—especially when circumstances remind us of our loss. Yet with God's grace, we come through to the other side. Despite our frailty, He carries us when we don't have the strength to continue forward. In the years to come, you will realize beauty and joy exist. Hope too. You have your best years in front of you."

"I know those are wise words, Eileen. It's not a straightforward journey, but I'm letting go and trusting God with my life. I don't understand why He closes a door, but He really knows best, doesn't He? I can rest in His love and grace."

Eileen traced the edge of the book with her fingers. "Good for you. Nothing we experience is wasted in the hands of an Almighty God. I appreciate Samuel's gesture, but if I had to live life all over again, I would still choose Rafe. I've also learned to thank God when He says no to me."

Debbie reached out and hugged her friend, the scent of sweet jasmine perfume lingering in the air. Eileen felt so frail and small, yet her faith remained bold and vibrant. Sensing the older woman needed to be alone, Debbie left the apartment. A quick backward glance revealed Eileen already lost in the novel, her voice a whisper as she read aloud.

After Debbie waved goodbye to Kim, who returned to her mother's room, she found Janet heading to the car. Beyond the sidewalk, a black Jaguar waited while the owner stood on the sidewalk. Hannah, as sweet as could be, approached Richard with a paper bag held out as perhaps a peace offering. Her buggy was parked next to the cars. No one else came with her, but it was a start. A new beginning.

If Debbie was a betting woman—and she wasn't—she'd guess a kuchen or some whoopie pies or half-moon pies, or samples of all three, lay carefully layered inside the bag. Richard appeared frozen to the sidewalk, his mouth dropping open in response to the gift.

Maybe someday Richard would reunite with the entire Lapp family. One could only hope.

As Debbie got into her car, Janet shot her a side glance. "Debbie, you are positively beaming!"

She gestured toward Hannah and Richard chatting together beneath the shade of a tall tree. "Do you see what I see? I texted Cheryl this morning and told her Richard was coming to Good Shepherd for a visit. She promised to call Lapp Lumber and let Hannah know."

Janet released a contented sigh. "Bless Hannah. She has a heart of gold."

Debbie had to agree. In the short time she had been back in Dennison, some of the most wonderful people she had ever encountered had offered friendship and support. God had led her on a wonderful journey, one that ordered her faltering steps. Who knew where He would lead her next?

"I'm blown away by Eileen's sweet spirit and her courage," Debbie said. "She's encouraged me, and you too. A week ago, I felt so overwhelmed with my to-do list. You and I have gone through plenty, between opening the café and then Annie turning out to be something we didn't expect. In fact, nothing has turned out as I expected. But I'm glad God brought us back together. You know what a massive change it's been for me, returning to Dennison and opening a new business, but there's no one else I would rather share this journey with."

Janet buckled her seat belt with a click. "Don't make me cry, Debbie Albright. I didn't wear waterproof mascara today. You know you're like a sister to me. We are on this adventure together, no matter what comes our way. I hope we have many more shenanigans in store."

Debbie grinned as she turned the ignition key. Outside her window, the sun shone, promising another lovely day to savor. As she drove to the Whistle Stop Café, she knew right down deep in her soul, there was no other place she would rather be.

Eileen was right. The best days were yet to come.

Dear Reader,

Thank you for joining me in Dennison, Ohio. It's possibly one of the most charming towns you'll ever visit. If you plan a trip, do head to the train station and tour the museum. You'll be inspired by the lives of the brave men and women who gave without reserve and who prized community and others above all else.

Chances are, *you* have a family member who might remember stories from World War II. It's worth collecting those memories to preserve for future generations. My paternal Irish grandfather fought during World War I. He later declared that he hoped he had fought enough so that his sons would never have to pick up a gun. My maternal grandfather emigrated from Norway to Canada. He deeply longed to serve in World War II, but because of health concerns and a lack of English language knowledge, he was forced to remain at home. He served in the best way he knew, working in the lumber camps, picking up English, and later serving as a pastor. I remember hearing about certain members of his Norwegian family joining the resistance, including one intrepid teenager who thwarted Nazi soldiers while hiding a radio inside a basket attached to his bike. The stories of the Greatest Generation continue to inspire and challenge. Everyone played an important role.

My Norwegian grandfather knew how it felt to be misunderstood, partly due to a language barrier, and also as a man who had no choice but to remain home. Both of my grandfathers inspired my idea of Samuel Lapp and Rafe Palmer and their burning desire to serve. Rafe Palmer, a war hero and half Italian, may have experienced both gratitude and misunderstanding from the public because of the anti-Italian sentiment at the time.

While most of the Amish stayed home from the war, many served in civilian public service projects, including work camps, and helped change hospital care by participating in medical research. Some of them harbored hard feelings for the separation from family and community. The more I researched Amish culture, the more I fell in love with it. You can dive into the plain life by reading Guideposts' previous series, Sugarcreek Amish Mysteries. I hope you enjoyed being reunited with the Sugarcreek heroines, Cheryl and Naomi, who solve exciting mysteries in the Amish community. Hannah and Naomi certainly represent the heart of the Amish. Faithful and ready to serve those in need. Quick to forgive. Willing to seek God's will, even if it means sacrifice.

Fun fact: Sugarcreek is only a hop away from Dennison.

Until next time,

Jenelle Hovde

## ABOUT the AUTHOR

enelle Hovde writes gentle stories of redemption and hope. She currently lives in Florida with her husband, close to the ocean for quick writing breaks. When she isn't writing, she homeschools three children and manages two spoiled cats who chase lizards. Her debut novel, *The Dream Weaver's Bride: Asenath's Story*, is a part of Guideposts' Ordinary Women of the Bible series, and she has written for other Guideposts series as well.

# A GLIMPSE of the PAST

**D**id soldiers' letters get lost in the mail?

The answer is yes. If you search the internet for "lost letters during World War II," you'll find some of the most romantic and tragic tales of lost loves or family. One of my favorite stories is about a son's letter to his mother that arrived seventy-five years after he sent it. The son's widow eventually received the note, thanks to the dedicated care of the US postal workers.

How did the government transport letters? During the First and Second World Wars, so many family members and loved ones wrote to their soldiers that the mail services quickly became inundated.

As a result, the V-mail system was implemented. Letters were microfilmed then transported to the military destination, where they were then increased to a readable size. This technique allowed massive amounts of paper documentation to be sent via cargo ships while protecting space for necessary equipment and supplies. After all, a ship couldn't contain solely mail! Soldiers used the V-mail for free, while Americans at home paid for the service. Censors worked to black out sensitive information in case of enemy interception.

Many young couples struggled to maintain long-distance relationships and keep the home fires burning. Unfortunately, plenty of soldiers received "Dear John" letters. Today, those soldiers' letters serve as a historical snapshot of a unique time. Some letters describe the storming of Normandy Beach, while others describe the conditions of war, allowing the reader into the soldier's heart and mind during a strenuous tour. Many letter writers celebrated the simple pleasures in life and begged for news about community, family, and friends.

It will be interesting to see how our current methods of corresponding will stand the test of time and if future generations will be able to read "lost" letters sent from soldiers overseas.

# FROM the HOME-FRONT KITCHEN

## Chocolate Whoopie Pies

**Ingredients:**

1 cup butter

2 cups brown sugar

4 eggs

2 teaspoons vanilla

3 cups all-purpose flour

1 cup cocoa

2 teaspoons salt

2 teaspoons baking soda

1 cup milk

**Filling Ingredients:**

1 egg white

2 teaspoons vanilla

2 teaspoons flour

2 teaspoons milk

2 cups confectioner's sugar

¾ cup Crisco

**Directions:**

Mix butter and brown sugar until creamy. Add eggs and vanilla. Mix flour, cocoa, salt, and baking soda and add to butter mixture alternately with milk. Drop onto baking sheet with cookie scoop or spoon. Bake at 350 degrees for 12 minutes.

**Filling Directions:**

Beat egg white until stiff. Add all other ingredients. Beat until smooth and fluffy. Once the cookies cool, drop filling with a cookie scoop in the middle of cookie and place another cookie on top. Press together lightly to spread filling toward edges. Wrap individually in plastic wrap. May be frozen.

*Read on for a sneak peek of another exciting book
in the Whistle Stop Café Mysteries series!*

# TILL THEN

## BY MARGARET WELCH

*L*ook at the crowd, and the program doesn't start for another
half hour," Janet Shaw said. "Kim should be happy."

"She'll be ecstatic," Debbie Albright agreed. "And I salute her
good sense in asking us to make cider and doughnuts." She turned
to the small boy standing at their new food cart. He wore a pint-size
World War II army uniform and a grin. "I salute you too." She held
her salute for a moment and then handed him a doughnut and cup
of cider. Between a quick sip and licking his lips he gave her a crisp
return salute, doughnut to forehead.

"It's About Time," the program that people flocked to this beautiful September Saturday, was the brainchild of the Dennison Railroad
Depot Museum's curator, Kim Smith. She'd invited all interested
citizens in the twin towns of Dennison and Uhrichsville, Ohio—
combined population not quite eight thousand—to celebrate the
recent discovery of a time capsule. Today, with the audience as wit-
nesses, she would open the time capsule that had not been touched
since it was sealed in 1950. Janet and Debbie, co-owners of the

Whistle Stop Café located in the Dennison Depot, were happy to do their part for the program's success. They'd closed the café at two, as usual, but Kim had hired them to provide cider and doughnuts for the program.

The crowd looked ready to take their role seriously and to celebrate. Like the small boy in his uniform, many wore styles honoring the World War II era the museum focused on. But Janet saw almost as many fifties-era poodle skirts along with bobby socks, saddle shoes, rolled jeans, and letter jackets in honor of the time capsule's creation date. She and Debbie wore aprons sewn from a 1940s pattern. Debbie's was pink-and-white gingham with red rickrack trim. Janet, who did the café's baking, went for an overall floral pattern.

"There goes a guy who didn't get the retro-fashion memo." Debbie nodded toward a gray-haired man wearing running shorts and skirting the growing crowd. "Not that there's a dress code."

"You know who that is, don't you?" Janet asked.

Debbie shook her head.

"Troy Henry. He's the one who found the time capsule and donated it to the museum. Or as Kim put it"—Janet made air quotes—"'*found*' it."

They watched as Troy Henry retraced his steps around the crowd and then pushed his way through it to the front where chairs were set up. He wasn't someone Janet had been aware of as she grew up, and that didn't surprise her. Troy was more than twenty years older than she was. Janet had returned to Dennison after college, though, and had since learned of his reputation.

"People say Troy always has an angle," she said. "Some of them call him 'Oh Joy.'"

"To his face?" Debbie asked.

"Apparently it doesn't bother him. That seems hard to believe though."

"I doubt you stoop to name-calling," Debbie said.

Janet smiled. "If he has a reputation and nickname like that, it makes me wonder what actual joy is missing in his life."

"Do you think Kim is wondering what his angle is in 'finding' the time capsule?"

"I don't know," Janet said, "but *I'm* wondering if she should have opened it alone, first, in case there's an unpleasant surprise inside."

"Everything ruined or something gross. Oh—" A vision of something just as bad crossed Debbie's face. "Or someone already got to it and the capsule is empty."

"Let's hope not, but Kim's taking a chance," Janet said. "It's weird how people lose track of time capsules, isn't it? They put all that effort into creating one. There's all the excitement and the hope of surprising future generations. Then it passes from memory, and it takes a renovation team or someone with a bulldozer to stumble across it again."

"But this one was tucked away in an old railroad safe," Debbie said. "A big honking thing, Kim says. The size of a large dorm refrigerator, at least. How do you lose something like that?"

"Out of sight and no way to set an alarm to remind anyone, I guess."

"No alarm that's foolproof or time proof, anyway."

The business partners and best friends had stationed their food cart in front of the café. Modeled after an ice cream cart, with wheels and a handle for easy pushing, pulling, and general maneuverability, the cart also had a canopy for sun protection. The body of the cart was a storage compartment with shelves for trays of pastries and room for beverages and a supply of paper goods and utensils. It was painted the same jaunty yellow that greeted people who walked through the café's front door.

Janet spotted Harry Franklin coming their way and waved.

Harry waved back and shuffled to the bench generally considered his because he occupied it so often in nice weather. Harry's canine pal, Crosby, kept pace with him. The elderly Black gentleman had started working for the railroad at age fifteen as a porter for the troop trains that came through Dennison during World War II. After the war, he became a conductor and stayed with the railroad until retirement. He wore his conductor's hat today, dressed for the occasion. Crosby looked alert and well-brushed, as always. He was a descendent of Bing, Dennison's famous World War I mascot—a decorated war hero.

"Want a doughnut and cider, Harry?" Debbie called.

"I'd like that." Harry started to get up.

"Stay right where you are, please. We deliver." Debbie took him a doughnut and cup of cider and apologized to Crosby for not patting his head. She went back to the cart and slipped on a new pair of plastic serving gloves. "The doughnuts are going like hotcakes. Do you think you made enough?"

"Oh ye of little faith," Janet said with the assurance she'd honed over her years working in bakeries. "We're fine and then some. I made three dozen more than Kim asked for."

The sound of raps on a door came over the museum's outdoor sound system, followed by the telltale scratchy sounds of a vintage record. "Come in!" a woman's pert voice called from the recording. "Well, well, well. Look who's here. I haven't seen you in many a year." The crowd hushed as the voice started singing "If I Knew You were Comin' I'd've Baked a Cake."

"Wow," Debbie said. "Does Kim know how to make an entrance or what?"

Kim Smith, in a 1950s shirtwaist dress, heels, and pearls—looking as put together as June Cleaver—rode out of the museum standing on an old, flat railroad freight wagon being pushed and pulled by four burly volunteers. Kim snapped the fingers of one hand to the lively entrance music and rested her other hand atop the time capsule container—the original Dennison Depot railroad safe. As the song ended and the volunteers brought the wagon to a stop, Kim echoed the last line, calling to the audience, "Howdya do, howdya do, howdya do?"

"Janet?" Debbie said over the crowd's roaring response.

"Hmm?" Janet, clapping as hard as anyone, had moved from behind the food cart and stood on her tiptoes to see Kim and the time capsule better.

"Go on over. I'll stay with the cart."

"You're sure?" Janet didn't argue when Debbie shooed her. She went to stand by Harry and Crosby.

"That," Kim told the audience with the aid of a cordless lapel mic, "was the 1950 recording of Eileen Barton singing the perfect song for today's celebration. Full disclosure, though"—Kim walked around the safe the way a magician might—"there's no guarantee we'll find anything recognizable or salvageable inside our time capsule. We only know, from a brief article that appeared in the *Evening Chronicle*, that, in 1950, a committee gathered the time-capsule materials and put them in a GI footlocker. The footlocker, in turn, was locked in this safe, which the railroad no longer used. To quote the article, 'the contents of the time capsule remain a mystery that will be revealed seventy years from now.'" Kim paused. "Now, of course it's been longer than seventy years, and we're late. What will we find inside? Do the items placed in a time capsule have an expiration date?" She walked around the safe again, studying each side. "The exterior is in surprisingly good condition, and that bodes well, so I'm willing to take a chance. How about you?"

As the crowd shouted agreement, Harry said to Janet, "That safe looks about as old as I do. As old as I feel anyway."

"Quite a bit *older* than you, Harry, and it could use some of your polish and shine. I'm going closer. Want to come?"

"You go on. Crosby and I got things covered here."

Janet took advantage of a space between two family groups and slipped past them. She found a place to stand behind the few rows of chairs, closer to the freight wagon.

"Isn't it amazing to think," Kim said, "that after creating the time capsule and locking it inside, they carted the whole kit and caboodle off to storage, where it was eventually forgotten? We didn't know it was lost, but now it's found."

"Why'd they choose seventy years?" came a shout from the crowd. "Why not fifty?"

"Or a hundred?" another voice called. "Seventy-five?"

"That's another mystery," Kim said. "Maybe something inside the time capsule will solve it."

"How you gonna open it?" someone else shouted. "Where'd you get the combination?"

"That 1950 newspaper article," Kim said. "It didn't say where the safe would be kept, but it did say where I could find the combination. So let's take a look inside, shall we?"

Kim twirled, making the full skirt of her dress swirl. She raised her right hand over her head and rubbed her fingertips together. Janet leaned forward, her breath held, while Kim entered the safe's combination with deft turns clockwise, counterclockwise, and clockwise again. She held up a pair of crossed fingers then turned the safe's T-bar handle and pulled the door open.

A shelf divided the safe's interior into upper and lower compartments, the lower being twice as tall as the upper. The green GI footlocker lay on the upper shelf, taking up the width of the shelf and most of its height. The lower compartment sat empty. The volunteers lifted a table and several archival boxes onto the wagon. Kim slipped on a pair of white cotton gloves, carefully took the footlocker from the safe, and set it at one end of the table.

"Well, it's light enough for me to move," Kim said. "So we know it isn't full of bricks."

The audience laughed.

"I'll stand beside the table, so I can face you," she continued. "That way you'll see what I'm doing. If all goes well, after cleaning and cataloging, we'll design a museum exhibit around the time capsule. So, although you won't get the best view of the contents today, we hope you will eventually."

"We can wait," a man yelled.

"Thank you," Kim said.

"No problem," the man replied. "We've already waited over seventy years."

Kim paused through the laughter then looked the footlocker over, describing it for the audience as she checked its condition. "Some military footlockers from the forties and fifties were leather. This one is metal. I see no rust. No signs of water damage. The newspaper article about it didn't say the committee locked the footlocker, and indeed it isn't. The hasps are stiff but move freely." She glanced up at the eager faces before her. "If I can take the items out without damaging them, I will, describing each one for you. The volunteers will repack them in these boxes. Anything that's too delicate or too far gone, I'll describe as best I can, but leave where it is. Ready? Moment of truth."

Kim lifted the lid then briefly put her hands to her lips. She started to speak but stopped. "Sorry," she said after a shuddering breath picked up by the mic. "I had no idea I'd get emotional." She gestured with both hands to the open footlocker. "Apart from yellowing paper, it could have been packed yesterday. There's an inventory list right on top. In case it's brittle, I'll slip a piece of archival paper underneath to support it as I take it out." A volunteer handed the archival paper to Kim, and she slid it under the inventory. "Oh, this is lovely. The inventory describes each item and the reason it was included. For instance, a list of Dennison High's straight-A students with the comment 'Our best and brightest—may their road to the future take them far, but if it takes them far away, may it bring them home often.'"

One by one, Kim took items from the footlocker. Some, like the list of A students, an essay detailing a day in the life of Dennison, and photographs and a newspaper article about the inaugural National Clay Week, were specific to the year 1950. The audience laughed over the 1950 town budget. Most of the items were memorabilia from town and depot history, including train schedules and copies of the *Evening Chronicle*, some with headlines on momentous dates. There were photographs that ranged from tintypes and sepia tones, to black and white and a few color images, and two ration books—one of them from Kim's mother, Eileen Palmer, and an unmarked, sealed envelope that Kim said they would have to open later. Janet's eye was particularly caught by a Betty Crocker booklet published in 1943 that featured recipes, menus, and hints on how to make meat, sugar, and other rationed foods go further.

After describing an advertising calendar from the T. Lanning and Company Department Store, Kim saw something in the footlocker that made her voice catch again. "Something I forgot to tell you is that we'll digitize the documents and photographs and make them available online. And…the recordings. Here's the last item, and it's a doozy."

She fanned herself before bringing the item out and describing it. "This is a round, flat tin about the size you'd have used to store a tape from one of those big old reel-to-reel recorders back in the day, which is exactly what's in here. There's a handwritten note on the lid. It says, 'Greetings from 1950. Recorded here are Dennison's elementary school children singing 'When You Wish Upon a Star' and the Community Church choir with 'The Sands of Time are Sinking.' These are followed by brief words of well-wishing from the mayor of our fair city, the honorable R.L. Roby. Our recording ends with Henry van Dyke Jr.'s poem 'Time Is,' recited by seventh-grade student Muriel Rau.'" Kim handed the tape tin to a volunteer. "We'll do our very best to make sure that everyone can hear the recording."

As Janet listened to Kim's closing remarks, she glanced at the safe then looked more closely. Was something else at the back of the top shelf? She couldn't be sure from where she stood, but she saw one empty chair closer to the freight wagon. She eased her way through the crowd, apologizing as she went until she could slip through the front line of chairs and claim the empty one. When she bumped into the chair to her right, she apologized one more time—to Troy Henry. Her apology didn't register, though, and she saw that his attention was also on the safe.

Troy nudged the man to his right and pointed to the safe. Janet couldn't hear if he said something, but the second man called out, interrupting Kim. "Something's still in the safe."

Kim checked the inventory. "Nothing else is listed."

"I don't know anything about that," the man said. "But something's in there. At the back."

From the look on Troy Henry's face, Janet was sure something was going on in his head too.

Did you love Debbie and Janet's visit to Sugarcreek? Want to know more about Cheryl Miller, the Swiss Miss, and the Amish? Well here's your chance! While you are waiting for the next fascinating story in the *Whistle Stop Café Mysteries*, check out this Guideposts mystery series!

## SUGARCREEK AMISH MYSTERIES

Pay a visit to the charming Swiss Miss gift shop in the village of Sugarcreek, known as the Little Switzerland of Ohio. You'll get to know Cheryl Cooper, a newly arrived "Englischer," who with her Siamese cat, Beau, is settling into the routine of running the store and adjusting to life in an Amish community. But it isn't the laid-back country living that Cheryl expects. She befriends Naomi Miller, an Amish farmer's wife, and together they lend a helping hand to their neighbors and untangle the mysteries of Sugarcreek.

*Blessings in Disguise*
*Where Hope Dwells*
*The Buggy before the Horse*
*A Season of Secrets*
*O Little Town of Sugarcreek*
*Off the Beaten Path*
*Peace Like a River*

*Simply Vanished*
*A Stitch in Time*
*Mason Jar Mayhem*
*When There's a Will*
*Shoo, Fly, Shoo!*
*Earthly Treasures*
*No Time for Trouble*
*All Abuzz at the Honey Bee*
*Home Sweet Sugarcreek*
*Blessed Are the Cheese Makers*
*Stranger Things Have Happened*
*In a Jam*
*A Play on Words*
*Digging Up Doubts*
*Horse Sense and Sensibility*
*A Tempting Taste of Mystery*
*To Have and to Hold*
*In the Fullness of Time*
*Home Fires Burning*
*Secrets Plain and Simple*
*Quilt by Association*
*Homespun Suspicions*
*Till We Meet Again*
*When Angels Whisper*
*Hark! The Herald Angel Falls*

**While you are waiting for the next fascinating story
in the *Whistle Stop Café Mysteries*, check out
some other Guideposts mystery series!**

# SAVANNAH SECRETS

Welcome to Savannah, Georgia, a picture-perfect Southern city known for its manicured parks, moss-covered oaks, and antebellum architecture. Walk down one of the cobblestone streets, and you'll come upon Magnolia Investigations. It is here where two friends have joined forces to unravel some of Savannah's deepest secrets. Tag along as clues are exposed, red herrings discarded, and thrilling surprises revealed. Find inspiration in the special bond between Meredith Bellefontaine and Julia Foley. Cheer the friends on as they listen to their hearts and rely on their faith to solve each new case that comes their way.

*The Hidden Gate*
*The Fallen Petal*
*Double Trouble*
*Whispering Bells*
*Where Time Stood Still*
*The Weight of Years*
*Willful Transgressions*

*Season's Meetings*
*Southern Fried Secrets*
*The Greatest of These*
*Patterns of Deception*
*The Waving Girl*
*Beneath a Dragon Moon*
*Garden Variety Crimes*
*Meant for Good*
*A Bone to Pick*
*Honeybees & Legacies*
*True Grits*
*Sapphire Secret*
*Jingle Bell Heist*
*Buried Secrets*
*A Puzzle of Pearls*
*Facing the Facts*
*Resurrecting Trouble*
*Forever and a Day*

# MYSTERIES OF
# MARTHA'S VINEYARD

Priscilla Latham Grant has inherited a lighthouse! So with not much more than a strong will and a sore heart, the recent widow says goodbye to her lifelong Kansas home and heads to the quaint and historic island of Martha's Vineyard, Massachusetts. There, she comes face-to-face with adventures, which include her trusty canine friend, Jake, three delightful cousins she didn't know she had, and Gerald O'Bannon, a handsome Coast Guard captain—plus head-scratching mysteries that crop up with surprising regularity.

*A Light in the Darkness*
*Like a Fish Out of Water*
*Adrift*
*Maiden of the Mist*
*Making Waves*
*Don't Rock the Boat*
*A Port in the Storm*
*Thicker Than Water*
*Swept Away*
*Bridge Over Troubled Waters*
*Smoke on the Water*
*Shifting Sands*

*Shark Bait*

*Seascape in Shadows*

*Storm Tide*

*Water Flows Uphill*

*Catch of the Day*

*Beyond the Sea*

*Wider Than an Ocean*

*Sheeps Passing in the Night*

*Sail Away Home*

*Waves of Doubt*

*Lifeline*

*Flotsam & Jetsam*

*Just Over the Horizon*

# MIRACLES & MYSTERIES
# OF MERCY HOSPITAL

Four talented women from very different walks of life witness the miracles happening around them at Mercy Hospital and soon become fast friends. Join Joy Atkins, Evelyn Perry, Anne Mabry, and Shirley Bashore as, together, they solve the puzzling mysteries that arise at this Charleston, South Carolina, historic hospital— rumored to be under the protection of a guardian angel. Come along as our quartet of faithful friends solve mysteries, stumble upon a few of the hospital's hidden and forgotten passageways, and discover historical treasures along the way! This fast-paced series is filled with inspiration, adventure, mystery, delightful humor, and loads of Southern charm!

*Where Mercy Begins*
*Prescription for Mystery*
*Angels Watching Over Me*
*A Change of Art*
*Conscious Decisions*
*Surrounded by Mercy*
*Broken Bonds*
*Mercy's Healing*

*To Heal a Heart*

*A Cross to Bear*

*Merciful Secrecy*

*Sunken Hopes*

*Hair Today, Gone Tomorrow*

*Pain Relief*

*Redeemed by Mercy*

*A Genius Solution*

*A Hard Pill to Swallow*

*Ill at Ease*

*'Twas the Clue Before Christmas*

# A NOTE FROM the EDITORS

We hope you enjoyed *Whistle Stop Café Mysteries series*, published by Guideposts. For over 75 years, Guideposts, a nonprofit organization, has been driven by a vision of a world filled with hope. We aspire to be the voice of a trusted friend, a friend who makes you feel more hopeful and connected.

By making a purchase from Guideposts, you join our community in touching millions of lives, inspiring them to believe that all things are possible through faith, hope, and prayer. Your continued support allows us to provide uplifting resources to those in need. Whether through our communities, websites, apps, or publications, we inspire our audiences, bring them together, and comfort, uplift, entertain, and guide them. Visit us at guideposts.org to learn more.

We would love to hear from you. Write us at Guideposts, P.O. Box 5815, Harlan, Iowa 51593 or call us at (800) 932-2145. Did you love *We'll Meet Again?* Leave a review for this product on guideposts.org/shop. Your feedback helps others in our community find relevant products.

*Find inspiration, find faith, find Guideposts.*

Shop our best sellers and favorites at

**guideposts.org/shop**

Or scan the QR code to go directly
to our Shop

# Find more inspiring stories in these best-loved Guideposts fiction series!

## Mysteries of Lancaster County

Follow the Classen sisters as they unravel clues and uncover hidden secrets in Mysteries of Lancaster County. As you get to know these women and their friends, you'll see how God brings each of them together for a fresh start in life.

## Secrets of Wayfarers Inn

Retired schoolteachers find themselves owners of an old warehouse-turned-inn that is filled with hidden passages, buried secrets, and stunning surprises that will set them on a course to puzzling mysteries from the Underground Railroad.

## Tearoom Mysteries Series

Mix one stately Victorian home, a charming lakeside town in Maine, and two adventurous cousins with a passion for tea and hospitality. Add a large scoop of intriguing mystery, and sprinkle generously with faith, family, and friends, and you have the recipe for *Tearoom Mysteries*.

## Ordinary Women of the Bible

Richly imagined stories—based on facts from the Bible—have all the plot twists and suspense of a great mystery, while bringing you fascinating insights on what it was like to be a woman living in the ancient world.

## To learn more about these books, visit Guideposts.org/Shop